One Grand Story

PRIMERS IN BIBLICAL AND THEOLOGICAL STUDIES
A Series from Codex Books

*One Holy Book: How the Bible Came to Be
and Why it Matters* (2021)

*One Grand Story: How the Bible Tells its Story
and Why it Matters* (2024)

"This new book on biblical theology hits the spot; actually, it hits the bullseye of two seldom achieved targets. Ched Spellman beautifully, accurately, and simply answers the two key questions: what? And so what? What does the believer need to know about God and his purposes for this world, and how does this make all the difference to how we live? Too often, only the first question is addressed. Spellman does not make this mistake. The result is a helpful book that will promote the importance and relevance of biblical theology to a new generation of readers."

—**Gregory Goswell**, Academic Dean and Lecturer in Old Testament, Christ College

"Spellman leaves the introductory reader in biblical theology spellbound. No word of a lie! He has an amazing gift for simplifying complex concepts. For anyone interested in going deeper into the Scriptures and seeking to understand the big picture as it is developed over the many small pictures provided by the text, for those who are interested in moving out of the trees of the forest to see the forest itself, this book is a real eye-opener. It comes with a practical guide to Christian living in light of the major biblical theology events and also includes a helpful resource for further study. Highly recommended!"

—**Stephen G. Dempster**, Emeritus Professor of Religious Studies, Crandall University

"Ched Spellman takes us on a fascinating fast-paced tour of biblical theology. He shows us what biblical theology is and why it matters by providing introductory chapters on the nature of biblical theology and by giving us representative examples of biblical theology at work. A pastoral spirit shines throughout the book, which also has a helpful bibliography of works to consult for further study. A helpful resource for students, teachers, and laypeople."

—**Thomas R. Schreiner**, professor of biblical theology, The Southern Baptist Theological Seminary

One Grand Story

How the Bible Tells its Story
and Why it Matters

Ched Spellman

Codex Books
Cedarville, OH

One Grand Story
How the Bible Tells its Story and Why it Matters

Codex Books
Cedarville, OH

First Edition 2024.

Printed in the United States of America

All bibliographic references utilize a shortened form.

Cover Image: Les Pélerins d'Emmaus (The Pilgrims of Emmaus), by Henry Ossawa Tanner, 1905. Public Domain.

Library of Congress Cataloguing-in-Publication Data

Name: Ched Spellman, author

Title: One Grand Story: How the Bible Tells its Story and Why it Matters

Description: Cedarville, OH: Codex Books, 2024. | Series: Primers in Biblical and Theological Studies | Includes bibliographical references and index.

Identifiers: ISBN: 978-1-7364459-2-1 (paperback)

Subjects: LCSH: Bible—Theology. LCSH: Hermeneutics—Religious aspects—Christianity.

For Mom

Contents

Introduction: Exploring our Textual Treasure   1

Part 1: How the Bible Tells its Story

1. The God Who Speaks
The Theological Basis for Biblical Theology   11

2. The Commissioned Storytellers
Biblical Authors and their Compositional Strategies   23

3. Grasping the Grand Storyline
How the Bible Is and Is Not a "Story"   39

4. Recognizing Canonical Signposts
Traversing the Bible's Literary Landscape   53

5. The Gospel of this Grand Storyline
The Depth & Dimensions of the Bible's Good News   67

6. The Great Hero of this Grand Storyline
Remembering the Risen Son of David   87

7. The Goal of this Grand Storyline
The Beginning and End of All Things   103

8. Life Between the Advents
Lord, Where are you Going?   113

9. Death Between the Advents
How Long, Oh Lord?   127

10. Your Story and His Story
Biblical Theology as a Way of Life   143

Part 2: Resources for Further Study

Books for Further Reading   161
Topics for Further Research   163
Glossary of Key Terms   173
Acknowledgments & Dedication   175
Scripture & General Index   177

Introduction

"The kingdom of heaven is like treasure, buried in a field, that a man found and reburied. Then in his joy he goes and sells everything he has and buys that field" (Matt 13:44).

"It does not do to leave a live dragon out of your calculations, if you live near him. Dragons may not have much real use for all their wealth, but they know it to an ounce as a rule, especially after long possession; and Smaug is no exception" (J. R. R. Tolkien, *The Hobbit*).

Exploring our Textual Treasure

The words of Scripture represent a gift beyond measure. In God's providence, Scripture is the means by which believers come to faith, grow in grace, and persevere to the end. In Scripture, the only true God speaks. By these words, the churches hear the word of God and are able to respond in truth to who God is and what God does. By God the Spirit, Scripture mediates the saving testimony to Jesus Christ who makes life with God the Father a reality.

These kinds of claims are just some of the features of what is often called a "high view" of Scripture. One of the reasons the churches should regularly teach and reflect upon their theology of Scripture is because there are often aspects of even the highest view of Scripture that can remain hidden.

J. R. R. Tolkien's book *The Hobbit* tells the tale of a hobbit, a wizard, and a group of dwarves who attempt to return to their kingdom under the Lonely Mountain. Standing in their way is a giant dragon named Smaug, who lives in the mountain and sleeps each night on top of their stolen treasure. As the dwarves contemplate the risk and reward of their mission, the narrator notes that "it does not do to leave a live dragon out of your calculations, if you live near him. Dragons may not have much real use for all their wealth, but they know it to an ounce as a rule, especially after long possession; and Smaug is no exception."

This scene provides a kind of analogy for some of the problematic ways that someone might relate the Scriptures and their personal practice.

On the one hand, someone might know the content of the biblical text but have no use for it. Like Smaug hovering over a priceless fortune, this person doesn't recognize the joyful burden and sober responsibility of the one who possesses this kind of wealth.

On the other hand, someone might appeal to the message of the Bible consistently but not really know it all that well. This person has some biblical knowledge but is not able to speak the language of the Scriptures fluently. They have made their find and purchased the field but never returned and explored the dimensions and proper use of their treasure.

Still others might know the Bible deeply and submit to its authority faithfully but have never considered the full scope of what they already believe about the Scriptures. These have a high view of Scripture and put it into practice in their life but would not be able to explain why that set of beliefs is coherent and accords with the meaning of those same Scriptures.

A constructive theological account of the nature of the Bible and the way it communicates its message can help motivate each of these types of people to grow in their understanding of how the Bible relates to the Christian life. This kind of study will help you to grasp the historical, textual, and theological responses to the question, "What is the Bible?"

Specifically, it not only helps you appreciate what is *in* the Bible but also what the Bible *is*.

As we will consider at length, what we believe about the Bible informs and is informed by a wide-ranging network of cherished beliefs.

It will not do to leave a living and active word out of our calculations!

Approaching the Text as a Biblical Theologian

Once we decide to explore this canonical treasure chest, what do we do next? Although studying the Bible requires a profoundly interdisciplinary approach, the discipline of biblical theology is uniquely suited to grapple with the message of the Bible as a whole.

"Biblical theology" is the careful study of the whole Bible on its own terms. Each element of this definition signals some of the distinctive tasks of biblical theology:

- *Careful study* recognizes that when we go about the task of biblical theology, we are utilizing a distinct set of literary tools and concepts. This kind of endeavor is not random or haphazard. The goal here is disciplined reflection on the biblical text rather than disordered analysis or random observations.

- *Whole Bible* indicates the key factor of "scope." In significant ways, biblical theology shares a family resemblance to exegesis (or close reading). In close reading, we typically focus in on a smaller unit of text and seek to understand and explain its meaning in its immediate literary context. Biblical theology is also "exegetical" because it seeks to understand and explain the meaning of biblical texts. One of the key differences is the size of the texts being examined. So, here the study of individual passages is brought alongside reflection on book-level meaning, the literary context of canonical sub-collections, and the effect of the Bible's two-testament shape.

- *On its own terms* signals that the primary goal of a biblical theology study is to explain the coherence and message of biblical passages and books using categories and frameworks that are in some way present and prominent in the texts themselves. What we choose to focus on here as biblical readers is guided by the choices of the biblical authors.

With this definition in place, you might understandably ask: How is biblical theology different from reading my Bible or doing any other type of theological reflection?

Exegesis (or close reading) is the study of an author's textual intention. How does the prophetic author, for example, use words, sentences, images, and themes to convey his message in this passage? *Theology* is the study of God and all things in relation to God according to his word. How does the prophetic author's message, for example, reveal God's character and purpose? And, what should we say today on the basis of what the prophets and apostles have said?

While these are distinct areas, the task of biblical theology requires you to utilize tools from each of these disciplines. When doing biblical theology, the goal is to first *present* the theological reflection that occurs *within* the Scriptures before *producing* theological reflection that *accords with* the Scriptures. Some "biblical theology moves" are closer to exegesis (like examining how one text draws upon another), and others are closer to theological reflection (like tracing a central theme across the biblical canon).

The Bible is an ancient collection of literary texts that reveals theological truth in a variety of genres. For this reason, it is profoundly unhelpful to pit these modes of study against one another (as if you could do one without at least some of the tools of the others!). The imperative move is to keep exegesis, biblical theology, and systematic theology *distinguished* but nevertheless *rightly related*.

How does Biblical Theology help me as a Believer and as a Bible Reader?

As we understand the discipline, the aim of biblical theology is to behold the big picture of the biblical writings and convey the inner workings of that big picture. How does the big picture of Genesis, for instance, relate to the big picture of the NT? Or, how does the book of Romans fit into the meaning of the rest of Paul's Letters?

Biblical theology tells a story from beginning to end. The story of the Bible begins with the Genesis creation account and ends with the outline of the "last things" in Revelation. These are the bookends of the grand storyline of the Bible.

In the beginning, God created the heavens and the earth, and in the end he makes a new heaven and a new earth. This cosmic scope is the staggering perspective that we encounter as we make our way through the biblical narratives, poems, prophecies, and epistles.

The perspective of biblical theology not only helps you as a biblical reader but also as a believer. The goal is not to fit the Bible's big picture into our little lives but rather to see our lives as a meaningful part of the world portrayed in the Bible.

If you are a believer, God in Christ and by the Spirit has opened your eyes and given you sight where once you were blind and wandering the world in spiritual darkness. Biblical theology, then, helps you adjust the prescription on the lenses through which you read the Bible and view the world.

There is so much to see!

How Can You Use This Book?

This book is a primer on the Bible's message as a whole and some of the most important tools that help us see this big picture. It includes a framework for biblical theology, an introduction to specific reading strategies, and also a series of biblical-theological reflections on key biblical themes. The goal is to display some of the *produce* of biblical theology but also to equip you with a working knowledge of the *process* of this kind of study as well.

In the first four chapters, I describe the theological and biblical basis for the study of biblical theology. God has chosen to reveal himself through inspired biblical authors who have written carefully crafted books. As part of a canonical collection, these biblical texts have a particular shape that includes a grand storyline of God's work in redemptive history.

In chapters 5–7, I reflect upon some of the central themes that show up and develop across the biblical canon (the gospel, the goal, and the great hero of this grand storyline). Chapters 8–10 then explore the way this big vision of the Bible's message informs the rhythm of our Christian lives (through joy, sorrow, life, and death).

In the final part of the book, I provide a series of resources for you to "dig deeper" in a given topic. In this section, there is an annotated list of books for further reading, a series of topics for further research in the academic discipline of biblical theology, and a brief glossary of key terms. This section of the book houses some of the technical details and conceptual tools mentioned or summarized in the main discussions in chapters 1–10.

These final features of the book are designed for it to function well as a supplementary textbook in an academic course in biblical or theological studies. At the end of each chapter, there are also reflection prompts and discussion questions. This resource is designed to facilitate small group discussion (either in a church or in a classroom setting).

Each of the topics I cover throughout this study has been discussed and debated at length in both academic and practical contexts. Footnotes tend to swarm around these topics and then dig in to build vast subterranean networks below the main text. I've tried (and *mostly* succeeded!) to omit scholarly debates, nuanced clarification, and other pedantic nonsense that I picked up from my training in "the academy," but I do want to acknowledge that many of the insights in this study have been honed by my teachers, colleagues, pastors, and students. Beyond this, further treatment of various topics in this volume and reference to the relevant scholarly discussions can be found in *Invitation to Biblical Theology* (Kregel, 2020).

Anyone that is familiar with biblical and theological studies might benefit from the broad approach and conclusions offered throughout this study. The primary purpose of these chapters, though, is to introduce the exciting study of biblical theology to those in classrooms (college and Seminary students) and local churches (pastors, lay leaders, church members, and casual readers).

The big idea of this little book is that biblical theology will help you navigate *the world of the biblical text*, and it will also help you locate yourself in *the biblical text's world*.

Brothers and sisters, press on!

Part 1

How the Bible Tells its Story
And Why it Matters

1

The God Who Speaks
The Theological Basis for Biblical Theology

What is the theological basis for envisioning the task of biblical theology as we have? More specifically, what is the theological foundation upon which we build our approach to reading the Bible and responding to God's work in the world?

Why Not Just Read the Text?

This line of questioning is important but sometimes neglected by readers of the Bible. In particular, those who rightly emphasize the importance of close textual analysis sometimes neglect (or worse!) deny that they are drawing on profoundly theological resources as they go about the task of biblical exegesis. "I'm just reading the text," one might say, "I don't need to bother with any theology."

This impulse is certainly understandable. Because we care about theology, it's sometimes tempting to come to a biblical text in search of support for a foregone theological conclusion. This mode of thinking is sometimes necessary and can be done well with careful analysis that is mindful of a given text's literary context. There are a host of assumptions, implications, and applications of biblical texts that can help us navigate our formulation of doctrine, our ethical judgments, and our cultural engagement. While affirming the importance of this contemporary application, the discipline of biblical theology maintains a prevailing focus on what biblical texts mean on their own terms. This kind of reading has enduring value as an end in itself.

Having said this, the attempt to avoid the embarrassment of "eisegesis" (reading meaning *into* a text rather than *out of* a text) does sometimes accelerate the pendulum swing in a different direction (away from an *overuse* of theology toward the potential *underuse* of theology). To avoid overly theoretical theologizing, some have simply sought to check their theological luggage at the gate (to be unpacked once they reach their exegetical destination).

This mindset, though, tends to mask just how much theology is involved when any reader seeks to "just read the text." Yes, significantly, the formal systematic procedure is safely stowed, but a substantive set of theological tools must still make up the contents of your carry-on.

For example, one might ask *why* it's so crucial to start with Scripture and maintain a textual focus. In response to this question, someone might rightly reason, "Because the Bible as a whole is God's authoritative word to his people, we should prioritize reading the text."

What the well-meaning student or scholar may not realize is that this is as loaded of a theological statement as you could make about the task of reading! I simply note here that a staggering set of assumptions is embedded within this simple starting point. "We should focus on the text" is a wonderful commitment, but it is also one that requires a robust theology of the Scriptures in order to make sense.[1]

A thoughtful doctrine of Scripture helps explain the confessional framework and motivation for the textual focus of both exegesis and biblical theology. Theological tools also help us reckon with the theological commitments that are always and already operative in the interpretive task.

For example, when a biblical reader takes for granted that the God mentioned in Genesis, Jeremiah, and Galatians all refer to the same being, this reveals an underlying assumption about the unity of the Bible's subject matter. In all of their historical diversity, their literary variation, and their theological focus, the texts of Scripture speak of one and the same God who is at work across the span of history. When we think carefully about the meaning of biblical texts (which will require textual tools), we must necessarily engage in theological reasoning (which will require theological tools).

In the end, we must grapple with theological categories because of the direction of the biblical authors themselves. In this sense, the use of theological tools can have an expressly exegetical motivation. The biblical authors compose narratives about the might of God's acts, but they also speak directly about the mystery of God's character.

As the psalmist declares, "You are good, and you do good" (Ps 119:68). David also reflects in this way by insisting that the Lord is "righteous in all his ways" and "faithful in all his acts" (Ps 145:17).

In the grand storyline of redemptive history, they insist, God speaks! The presence of both accounts of divine action and communication of divine speech means that our approach to reading the Bible must include historical awareness, literary sensitivity, and theological precision.

History & His Story

As noted above, the task of biblical theology requires a theological framework in theory and also utilizes theological tools in practice. In the rest of this chapter, we will explore just some of the theological categories that are particularly relevant to our approach to studying the whole Bible on its own terms.

Biblical theology begins with the most basic commitment of Christian theology. The God of the Bible is the God of creation and providence. While distinct, these concepts have a close interrelation. Because he created and fashioned all things, he therefore rules and reigns over all things. This theology of creation encompasses both origin and intention. God produces the world with the power of his words (Gen 1:1ff; Heb 11:3) and orders all things with the purpose of his will (Gen 2:15; Isa 43:7; Eph 1:9–10).

These doctrines of creation and providence are the bedrock upon which biblical theology finds its footing. The grand storyline of the Bible opens at the beginning of all things and closes with a future vision of the end of days.

A straightforward reception of the Bible's narrative scope, then, requires the theological notions that God himself is the origin of all things and is somehow bringing all of history to a meaningful end.

All of *history*, in other words, is *his story*.

God's Word Spoken & God's Word Written

The next step in the program of biblical theology requires not only a general affirmation of God's creative purpose but also a specific articulation of God's special revelation. The existence of God's purpose requires divine power and initiative. Knowledge of this purpose requires the miracle of divine revelation.

Chief among our theological commitments is that God is a communicative being who has in fact chosen to reveal himself and his will for humanity. This revelation occurs through a divine display in the created order (general revelation) and through divine discourse in covenant relationships (special revelation).

Wonder upon wonder, the God who created all things chose to communicate to those creatures. In the grand storyline of the Bible, God speaks. As Francis Schaeffer would say, "He is there. And he is not silent." This divine speech is the means by which God creates the world and also covenants with his image-bearing people. The creation account in Gen 1–2 lays the theological groundwork for the claim that God's words give life and enact the divine-human encounter of covenant.

The *God of creation* is also the *God of the covenants*.

Accordingly, any ultimate account of this world must consider both the story of creation and the concept of covenant. It must reckon with both revelation and redemption.

The possibility of biblical theology requires not only an affirmation that God speaks, but also an affirmation that this divine discourse can be communicated through human words and written texts. An exegetical approach to biblical theology that focuses on the meaning of biblical texts requires a robust theology of written revelation.

Scripture as a Feature of God's Gracious Design

An approach to biblical theology that is rooted in the canonical writings further relies on the affirmation that God's special revelation is located in the written texts of Scripture by his gracious design.

A high view of Scripture includes the affirmation that the biblical texts are collectively the Word of God. The doctrine of Scripture examines what we say about what God says. Central to this confessional position is the relationship between God's word spoken and God's word written.

A working definition of Scripture is *God's word to his people*. To unpack this definition fully requires that we say something theological (*God's*), hermeneutical (*word*), and historical (*to his people*). A theology of the Scriptures also examines what we say about when, where, and how God speaks.

Throughout the biblical canon, statements are made about God's speech that draw a close connection between who God is and what God does through his words. In some of the most important biblical texts for the doctrine of Scripture, Peter and Paul make an important link between God's word spoken and God's word written (2 Pet 1:16–21; 2 Tim 3:14–17).

What's more, within the Scriptures themselves there are also several narratives that portray the work of authors, the production and theological significance of texts, and the pivotal role of readers. Even a quick overview of these instances can help strengthen the conviction that the prominence of written texts is intentional rather than incidental in God's plan of redemption.

Narrative Portrayal of Authors, Texts, and Readers in the OT & NT

One of the most significant portrayals of God's word spoken and God's word written occurs after the exodus at Mount Sinai (Exod 19–24). Here God himself inscribes his words upon stone tablets that are then read by Moses and received by the people as the words of the Lord. At the end of his life, Moses compiles and composes the "book of Moses" that then functions as an authoritative account of God's actions and will for Israel (Deut 30–34).

As they encounter and interpret God's actions in the judgment of exile, the prophets compose their books in light of the book of Moses. In the book of Jeremiah, the prophet speaks God's words of impending judgment and future deliverance. In a dramatic and instructive scene toward the middle of this prophetic book, Jeremiah receives a direct word from the Lord and delivers it to the king of Israel through a lengthy process including Baruch the scribe, a copied scroll, court officials, and rewritten texts (Jer 36:1–32).

In both of these scenes from redemptive history, God himself speaks and also specifies that his spoken communication would be delivered by means of written texts. The biblical authors of these scenes also take care to trace the link between God's word spoken and God's word written. As readers, we hear God's speech, we see the prophetic composition of the text, we follow the transmission of the text across time and into new locations, we hear the words read aloud, and we witness others receive or reject these words as God's word.

In the NT, the preaching of Jesus Christ during his incarnation represents a special moment in redemptive history. Here the incarnate Word speaks and teaches about who God is and the meaning of his own work of redemption. Through commissioned disciples, the gospel is preached in the earliest churches after Jesus's death, resurrection, and ascension. Significantly, the four Gospels anticipate the transition from the gospel preached to the Gospels written.

The "gospel of the kingdom" is initially proclaimed *by* Jesus (Matt 4:23; 9:25), the gospel is then declared *about* Jesus (Matt 26:13; 1 Cor 15:3–4), and then the term "Gospel" eventually indicates the biblical books that recount both the message Jesus proclaimed and the message proclaimed about him (Matt 1:1; Jn 21:24–25). In their letters to the churches, the NT authors also anticipate that their written texts would be the means by which future generations of readers would encounter God's special revelation (1 Thess 2:13; 2 Pet 3:15–16).

The opening sequence of Mark's Gospel illustrates this profound and theologically explosive dynamic between divine discourse and written texts. The narrative action begins with John the Baptist's prophetic speech about the coming of Christ (Mk 1:4–8). The next instance of speech is the divine voice of the Father from the heavens directed at Jesus himself, "You are my beloved Son; with you I am well-pleased" (Mk 1:11). Significantly, the next spoken words in this opening sequence are Jesus's own proclamation of the "gospel of God," which he summarizes by saying, "The time is fulfilled, and the kingdom of God is at hand; repent and believe in the gospel" (Mk 1:15).

In the context of these spoken words, Mark characterizes his written text as a whole with a heading that indicates what the book will be about (Jesus, the Christ) and how it is supposed to function (as proclaimed "good news"). Mark indicates that this opening section is "the beginning of the gospel of Jesus Christ, the Son of God" (Mk 1:1). This written text will be how the good news of Jesus will be proclaimed and heard by future generations.

Much more could be said about these texts and the theological implications of these narratives. For our purpose, though, they each demonstrate that the writing of the Bible is a prominent part of the Bible itself. This textual feature should give us confidence in an approach that assigns written texts a normative role in both our method of interpretation and our mode of presentation.

The God Beyond Knowing Who Has Made Himself Known

In this chapter, we have discussed some of the theological basis for the study of biblical theology. Central here to the study of the Bible's witness to God himself is a deep theological truth in a Christian theology of revelation: that God is both *ultimately incomprehensible* and yet *graciously knowable*.

Both of these elements must be operative in our theological method if we are going to rightly speak about the God spoken of in the Scriptures.

Late in his massive work, *Against Heresies,* early church leader Irenaeus addresses both incomprehensibility and knowability. This is an important maneuver in light of who he is seeking to refute: false teachers who prioritized both secret knowledge and also the impossibility of truly knowing anything about the transcendent God(s).

He writes, "The Lord taught us that no man is capable of knowing God, unless he be taught of God; that is, that God cannot be known without God."[2]

This is the sanctifying dynamic that inescapably engulfs theological discourse. True knowledge of God is beyond our comprehension, but this too is known only through special revelation.

Had God not chosen to reveal himself, we would have no knowledge of him.

The *revelation* of *incomprehensibility* both grounds and governs the possibility and limitations of our theological god-talk. This dynamic is not an intellectual language game but a paradox at the burning core of all theology.

Part of everything God has revealed is that he has not revealed everything about God.

Our theological confidence and discursive efforts are supposed to bend to this economic reality. Brain-breaking though it should seem, the outer reach of incomprehensibility balances the immersion of knowability. This should generate both boldness *and* humility in the biblical theologian.

The two-fold thesis for incomprehensibility and knowability is Deut 29:29: "The secret things belong to the Lord our God," so this means he keeps secrets and will never be exhaustively known outside of himself. This should deeply humble us.

Who among us could speak of the unspeakable?

"But the things that are revealed belong to us and to our children forever," so this means that by grace alone we can trust God's testimony about himself. This should deeply embolden us.

Who among us could refrain from speaking of the one who has given us words to say?

The Christian theologian is tasked with the impossible task: Speak rightly of the one who is ineffable.

His "greatness is unsearchable" (Ps 145:3), the psalmist declares. Now search out his greatness, the psalmist demands.

This is part of the impossibility that the advent of the Son makes possible. With an economy of words, the Word has made known the divine economy. In these last days, God has spoken to us "by his Son" (Heb 1:1).

He gave men and women of this world the ability to say, "Glory to God in the highest."

A wondrous gift indeed!

On the basis of this gift of revelation and redemption, the believing churches can pursue the task of biblical theology.

Discussion & Reflection:

1. What has been your experience with the kind of "biblical theology" described in this book so far? Do you default to thinking about the "big picture" of the Bible's message, or do you typically focus on the "little picture" of specific truths or individual passages?

2. What is happening when you read the Bible? If someone says that they don't need to think about any theology because they are just "reading the text," how might you help them see some of the theological truths they are assuming or affirming when they commit to reading the Scriptures?

3. What effect would it have on your theology of the Scripture and the Christian life if you denied or downplayed either God's incomprehensibility or his knowability?

Notes:

1. Some of these assumptions would be 1) that God exists, 2) that he exists as a communicative being, 3) that he has created a world with creatures capable of receiving divine revelation, 4) that he has in fact chosen to reveal himself, 5) that human words can convey meaning and truth adequately, and 6) that the written texts of Scripture are an adequate medium of divine discourse.
2. Irenaeus, *AH*, 4.6.4 as cited in Spellman, *Irenaeus: Essential Writings* (Fontes Press, 2023).

2

The Commissioned Storytellers
Biblical Authors and Their Textual Strategies

In the last chapter, we examined the *confessional* aspect of our approach to biblical theology. A strong theology of the Scriptures convinces us that the words of the Bible in part and on the whole are God's word to his people. All texts have authors, and biblical texts have prophetic authors who by the Spirit of God have written texts that communicate to us the message that God intends for us to understand.

In this chapter, we focus on the *compositional* aspect of our approach to biblical theology. Encountering God's special revelation in the Scriptures is an inescapably *textual* task. After affirming *that* God has chosen to communicate his special revelation to us through inspired prophets and apostles, we can now ask *how* these authors went about their work. How have the biblical authors put their texts together? How did they communicate their theological message?

Now, someone might ask at this point, Isn't this obvious? Why specify that you're taking a "textual" approach to reading? Is this some form of redundant repetition or tortured tautology?[1] "The best approach to reading words is to read the words." Wow, great insight! Well, remarkably, there are a host of ways to read a text (and biblical texts in particular) that draw attention to an array of interesting but ultimately external elements.

For example, someone who loves history and thinks about the Roman Empire every day might be inclined to mine the NT writings for any connection to the broader sweep of Greco-Roman history. Someone else might comb through the Psalms to find verses that help support one of God's attributes. Another might read through OT narratives in search of examples that illustrate a particular vice or virtue. Still another might read a verse each morning in order to find practical wisdom for that coming day.

A focus on the "textual features" of a biblical writing does not actually exclude any of these historical, theological, ethical, or devotional aspects of the Bible's meaning. In a textual approach, though, we're prioritizing the literary elements by which an author has composed the text.

We are also trying to reckon with the nature of our object of study: written acts of communication. While mindful of the historical and social elements involved in this task, we're homing in on the textual intention of biblical writers.

The prevailing question for reading thus becomes, "What has the author communicated *in just these words* written *in just this way*?" Recognizing the way an author has written his text will aid us as we read that same text.

In other words, a "compositional approach" to reading seeks to follow the path that the author has laid out for us. Any kind of further significance of these texts should be shaped by the author's handiwork.

The Biblical Authors Knew What They Were Doing

A foundational assumption here is that the biblical writers were competent authors that had discernible purposes in their written texts.

In other words, they knew what they were doing.

This is why it's appropriate to speak of an author's "compositional strategy" or purpose in writing. When we ask where an author has led us, we are assuming that this given writer has actually created a path!

The biblical writings are not literary grab bags or notebooks filled with a disjointed series of meandering messages. They are carefully crafted texts that harness a variety of textual features to make their direct, subtle, and profound points.

Biblical narratives are engaging because they tell their stories with unfolding drama, interesting characters, and plots that twist and turn in often unexpected ways. Hebrew poetry sinks and soars with images, emotions, and analogies that paint brilliant and haunting portraits of God and his world. NT epistles brim with theological insight and compelling rhetoric. Proverbs make us pause and ponder, parables set us on the pursuit of meaning, dialogues allow us to overhear, and prophetic visions give us so much to see!

The biblical writings are what they are because of the choices that their competent authors make as they skillfully compose their texts. Acknowledging these features allow us to recognize *both* the theological depth of the Scriptures and also their literary artistry.

Biblical texts are not like newspapers, which you read for specific information that is quickly out of date. If you meditated day and night on a single entry for the *New York Times*, we might question your reading comprehension skills.

Biblical texts are much more like layered and complex works of art. You can usually immediately see what a portrait, painting, or sculpture depicts, but if you maintain your gaze, you'll deepen your appreciation for the details that make it what it is. Biblical authors have communicated their message in a way that can be understood directly but can also reward a lifetime of careful study.

The Biblical Authors Wrote Books by Design

An author's textual intention is seen most fully at the book level of composition. In other words, while it is often appropriate to focus on an individual section or a portion of a biblical book for a given study, project, or sermon, the meaning of that passage or section is governed and guided by the meaning of the book as a whole.

In addition to interpreting the words, sentences, and phrases of a passage, we also want to be aware of the proper context necessary to understand the meaning of that passage. The close reading of a particular passage is best complemented by an understanding of its surrounding literary context (i.e., paragraphs, larger sections, and blocks of discourse). The reader ultimately aims to see how a particular passage functions in light of the book in which it appears.

The goal here is to notice any textual connections that an author makes within a single biblical book. This level of analysis is *inner-textual*, as it analyzes the relationship between the various parts of a particular text within the scope of the work itself. This approach to exegesis or close reading emphasizes book-level meaning as the proper context in which an individual passage functions.

To give just one quick example, consider the biblical books whose message would be characterized very differently without taking into account their beginning or end. When reading Jonah 1–3, it would be possible to surmise that the reason Jonah flees to Tarshish is because he fears that the people of Nineveh will *fail* to listen and repent (i.e., he wants them to hear and experience deliverance). In Jonah 4, however, this interpretation is ruled out as Jonah explicitly states that he fled because he feared that the people of Nineveh would *in fact* listen and repent (i.e., he wants them to reject the message and experience judgment). Because of his knowledge of God's character, Jonah knew that the Lord would relent and deliver them (Jonah 4:1–3). This leads to an articulation of the theme of the book as a whole: God's sovereign freedom to execute judgment and extend mercy.

This theme resonates with the broader context of the Book of the Twelve and connects with the character of God developed in strategic texts in the Pentateuch (e.g., Exodus 34). Only a book-level reading of Jonah's narrative as a whole is capable of discerning this aspect of the author's theological purpose and perceiving the book's connection to broader biblical-theological themes.[2]

This simple hermeneutical guideline allows a biblical author to direct our focus when we seek to reflect upon his purpose in writing or summarize the theological message of his book.

This way of keeping the book-level meaning in view also prepares us for any biblical-theological analysis that involves the relationship between the messages of two or more biblical books.

The Biblical Authors Were Also Biblical Readers

One of the most important ways for us to see how the Bible fits together is to observe the web of intertextual connections that are woven into the fabric of biblical books, that hold together canonical collections, and that help establish the two-testament coherent shape of the Christian Bible as a whole.

Biblical intertextuality is the study of the relationship between two or more biblical texts. More specifically, biblical intertextuality focuses on the connections that are a part of a biblical author's textual intention. This type of study is challenging, but it's also among the most fruitful tasks you could focus on as a student of the Bible. Indeed, one of the distinctive elements of biblical writings is their pervasive and profound use of other texts.

The biblical *writers* were also biblical *readers*.

When you begin to recognize the circuitry of this intertextual network as you read, you will be able to appreciate the deep structure of the Bible's intricate and interlocking message.

Sometimes these connections are directly noted (like *quotations* of other texts), sometimes they are indirectly cited (like *allusions* to a phrase or theme), and other times they are subtly woven into an author's presentation (like an *echo* of an OT story's plot structure).

To give an example of each of these types of intertextual connections in close proximity, we can briefly consider the first chapter of Mark's Gospel. After a direct opening ("The beginning of the gospel of Jesus Christ, the Son of God," Mk 1:1), Mark uses a *quotation* from Mal 3:1 and Isa 40:3. He introduces the blended quotation by saying, "As it is written in Isaiah the prophet" (Mk 1:2).

Following the conclusion of his brief baptism account, Mark describes how a voice from heaven declares, "You are my beloved Son; with you I am well pleased" (1:11). Here, Mark makes an *allusion* to Ps 2:7 and Isa 42:1, as the words recorded in this declaration from the Father indirectly reference the words of this poetry and prophecy.

The opening chapter of Mark's Gospel ends with the temptation account where Jesus "was in the wilderness forty days, being tempted by Satan" (1:13). Unlike the temptation accounts of Matthew and Luke, Mark adds the unique detail that while he was in the wilderness Jesus "was with the wild animals, and the angels were ministering to him" (1:13). This detail is a possible *echo* of several biblical narratives that describe Israel being tested in the wilderness where there were also wild animals (e.g., Deut 7–8, esp. 7:22 and 8:15; Ezek 34:5).

These three main types of intertextual connections can equip you to see what a biblical author is doing in a biblical text. While Mark's opening stretch of narrative will make sense even if you overlook these references, reckoning with the presence of these connections is like restoring the intertextual electricity to a messianic floodlight that illuminates the person and work of Jesus as the Christ.

Sometimes an intertextual reference supports the author's argument; sometimes it serves as a point of contrast or an illustration. Sometimes it is simple; sometimes it is complex. Sometimes it is difficult to discern exactly what a biblical author intended in the use of an intertextual link.

The intertextual practice of the biblical authors is diverse but consistent. If they have utilized another biblical text, you can be certain that they have a reason (a "textual intention"), and our role as readers is to discern that purpose in their writing.

This last step of intertextual analysis returns to the point of departure and asks what impact the intertextual payload made when it entered the atmosphere of the passage at hand. The key question here is, "How is the meaning of this passage informed by the meaning of the text that has been cited?"

Some of the most memorable "aha" moments that you will encounter will occur as you trace these kinds of intertextual connections between biblical passages.

Though this chapter has included perhaps the most technical section of this book, it describes the critical substructure that supports all of the other biblical-theological moves we might make.

To sum up this section, a compositional approach to studying the Bible draws together several significant horizons of reading: that the biblical authors "knew what they were doing" (*textuality*), that they "wrote books by design" (*inner-textuality*), and that they were themselves "biblical readers" (*inter-textuality*).

Letting the Author Lead:
Oh the Places You'll Go!

Biblical theology aims to articulate the "big picture" of the Bible. It also seeks to think carefully about the themes that show up and develop across the biblical canon. Because our approach to biblical theology is geared to the study of the Bible on its own terms, this chapter's reminders are crucial.

It's remarkably easy to take a road trip with a biblical theme or the Bible's "overarching message" that leaves individual biblical texts with their granular details and their distinctive patterns in the rearview mirror.

The textual anchor of the inspired author's compositional strategy can keep our theological reflection from drifting toward the undertows of eisegesis and the currents of passing cultural storms.

This may seem unduly restrictive for someone who believes that all of Scripture is inspired by the Holy Spirit. My suggestion, though, is that the commitment to following the contours of the biblical text does not lead you to a new destination, but it often takes you on a different route to get there!

This discussion is particularly relevant when you're presenting the meaning of a biblical passage in a lesson, sermon, or devotional context.

How does the "big picture" of the Bible relate to the "little picture" of a given biblical text?

Should You Make a Beeline for the Cross?

Let's consider perhaps the most important and precious theological conviction of the Christian church: The Bible is about Christ. All of it.

This theological commitment is the centerpiece of most Christian teaching about the meaning and message of the Bible as a whole.

The issue we're examining at this point is not *that* the Bible is about Christ but rather *how* the Bible is about Christ. Those that share the foundational belief that the Bible is about Christ often differ about the best way to understand this claim.

Convinced that the whole Bible is about Christ, sometimes a reader might seek to quickly move from the passage being read to its Christological sense, or simply speed up the storyline to get to Christ. This raises the question in another way: If the whole Bible is about Christ, should we look for Christ in every passage and make him the focus of every sermon in the same fashion?

In 1859, Charles H. Spurgeon preached a sermon called "Christ Precious to Believers." In this sermon, Spurgeon includes an anecdote from a Welsh minister. In this anecdote, a young preacher gives a sermon and receives feedback from an older minister. The older minister critiques his "very poor sermon" not because of his explanation of the text, which he found very good, but rather because "there was no Christ in it."

The younger preacher answers that, "Christ was not in the text; we are not to be preaching Christ always, we must preach what is in the text." The older minister responds,

"Don't you know, young man, that from every town, and every village, and every little hamlet in England, wherever it may be, there is a road to London?" After the young preacher agrees, the older minister concludes:

And so from every text in Scripture, there is a road to the metropolis of the Scriptures, that is Christ. And my dear brother, your business is when you get to a text, to say, 'Now what is the road to Christ?' and then preach a sermon, running along the road towards the great metropolis— Christ. And . . . I have never yet found a text that had not got a road to Christ in it, and if I ever do find one that has not a road to Christ in it, I will make one; I will go over hedge and ditch but I would get at my Master, for the sermon cannot do any good unless there is a savour of Christ in it.[3]

Spurgeon's anecdote is a vibrant illustration which, in typical Spurgeon fashion, clearly communicates the powerful impact of preaching Christ.

While the above anecdote is helpful, though, it is also susceptible to a kind of misuse. As believers, we have warrant and motivation to preach Christ "from every text in Scripture."

The issue, however, is not theological (i.e., *that* Christ is worthy to be preached and the goal of Scripture) but hermeneutical: *How* is Christ to be understood and proclaimed "from every text in Scripture" that does justice to every text in Scripture?

In Spurgeon's illustration, the Scriptures are envisioned as a network of towns, villages, and hamlets scattered across

England. They are disconnected from one another, but all have a road that leads to the central metropolis of the country: London. In the same way, each text of Scripture has a "road toward the great metropolis—Christ."

When you encounter a text in this approach, you must eventually run toward the great Christological metropolis. Most pointedly, this method is applied to every passage and every sermon: "I have never yet found a text that had not got a road to Christ in it, and if I ever do find one that has not a road to Christ in it, I will make one."

Making a Beeline That Follows a Storyline

Sometimes this hermeneutical and homiletical technique is paraphrased and attributed to Spurgeon as, "I take my text and make a beeline for the cross." When used without careful reflection, this phrase can become a hermeneutical principle that influences the way a reader reads and a preacher preaches.

How might the approach to biblical theology that we have already discussed inform this particular issue of reading and preaching?

The "biblical theology move" we might make is to look a little closer at the textual paths we're taking in this theological journey. Before we can ask how the whole Bible points to Jesus, we must ask how the whole Bible itself fits together.

Knowing what the Bible as a whole is about and how it fits together is an inestimably valuable aid for seeing how it all leads to Jesus as the Christ.

The biblical authors have laid out a textual journey for their readers to follow. Our goal as biblical theologians is to follow these authors and ask what they are up to. How has an author directed us to think a certain way or to interpret an event, a concept, or a theme? In other words, the Spurgeon illustration actually turns out to be useful, if thought out a little further.

In this scenario, it is not that every text has a special dedicated road that leads only to Christ. Rather, every text is part of a complex but orderly system of roads that ultimately leads to Christ. Further, those roads are often interconnected. Just as the towns, villages, and hamlets of England possess roads that lead to London, they also have roads that connect to one another.

The key difference here is that the paths of the Scriptures are not simply byways for vagabond travelers but are more like roads that have been plotted on a carefully designed roadmap that we have access to. This textual transportation system consists of books, groupings, two Testaments, and a narrative storyline signposted by a series of covenants. The final part of the Spurgeon illustration, then, is where the biblical theologian would get off the train.

For the biblical theologian, the role of the reader is never *to make* a path to Christ, but always *to follow* the path to Christ that the biblical authors have laid down.

This route requires patience, but only the patience necessary to get you to the text. Once you are there, your journey awaits. There you will find the biblical author waiting, revealing God in Christ to you by the Spirit.

The grand storyline of the Bible and its network of covenant promises and expectations find their end in Christ. This path is long and winding, but will lead you to the theological richness of your destination. This line is not as the crow flies, but is the one where the cross lies. Taking a canonical line to the cross may not be straight or fast, but it's true.

The discipline of biblical theology aims to navigate this balance of unity and diversity. The gospel of Jesus Christ is to be proclaimed from all of the Scriptures. The gospel according to Genesis will have a different shape, tone, and feel than the gospel according to Galatians.

This sensitivity to the details of the biblical texts, the theological developments of the biblical storyline, and the unity of God's work in the divine plan of redemption will ably equip us to reckon with the gospel wherever we might find ourselves in our travels to and fro across the literary landscape of the biblical canon.

Discussion & Reflection:

1. What difference do you think it makes to consider what biblical authors are intending in their texts? How might the question, "What is this biblical writer up to?" connect to the question, "How does this biblical passage apply to me?"

2. Why is it important to keep your eye on the message of a book as a whole? How would you describe the message of chapters 1–3 of the book of Jonah? Have you ever heard Jonah's story summarized like this? What would change about the main point if Jonah 4 is also included?

3. What do you think about Spurgeon's illustration about making a beeline for the cross in every sermon, lesson, or discipleship conversation? Do you agree completely? Think it should be modified? Perhaps rejected? Regardless of which response you chose, what role do you think biblical theology plays in answering this question?

Notes:

1. One of the best entries of the xkcd webcomic is called "Honor Societies," which ends with an orientation session scene with the leader explaining, "Listen up! The first rule of tautology club is the first rule of tautology club."
2. A few other examples where the critical hermeneutical significance of book-level meaning can be seen is the narrative bookends of Job (in relation to the pointed dialogue that occurs in the bulk of the book) and the final thesis statement of Ecclesiastes (imagine all the various ways you might misconstrue the main purpose of this wandering discourse without the concluding statement of 12:13!).
3. For the text of this sermon, see Charles Spurgeon, "Christ Precious to Believers," The Spurgeon Archive, Midwestern Baptist Theological Seminary, http://archive.spurgeon.org/sermons/0242.php.

3

Grasping the Grand Storyline
The Canonical Shape of Redemptive History

Being able to recognize and articulate the story found in the Scriptures is crucial for understanding how the Bible fits together as a whole. One of the means by which the biblical canon shapes the expectations of its readers is the way that it frames the biblical meta-narrative and situates the prophetic and apostolic discourse in the larger storyline.

How the Bible Is and Is Not a "Story"

Do you see a problem here yet? Especially in light of our discussion in previous chapters on the meaning of individual texts and the strategic significance of biblical books, you might sense a bit of tension with the idea that the Bible is "one grand story" that speaks of Christ. In order to see how the Bible is a story that leads to Christ, we need to consider the ways in which the Bible is *not* one story. As you may have guessed, it's important to clarify what we mean when we speak of the "biblical metanarrative" or the "grand storyline of the Bible."

Imagine that you're a new believer and also a new Bible reader. You hear someone say that the Bible is a unified story that speaks of the good news about Jesus. You also hear that it's imperative to read and reread the Bible, so you get started at the beginning in Gen 1. After reading about the creation of the world, a global flood, and the tower of Babel with its host of nations listed, you think that this story is about events on a worldwide scale. In Gen 12 you get a little whiplash as the story zooms in on a single family. In Gen 1–11, we moved through time like a bullet train, but now large sections of text make their way through only a handful of generations (chapters 37–50 on Joseph!).

After a lengthy gap of time, the action picks up again with Moses and the dramatic conflict with Pharaoh and Egypt. The people finally escape through the miraculously parted waters and make their way to Mount Sinai to hear from the Lord. The pace of the story has picked up. We're seeing God's mighty acts and a strong forward progression. When the Israelites arrive at the foot of the mountain, though, this narrative action comes to a screeching halt.

The chronological time covered is brief here (around a year), but the textual space devoted to this time is enormous! The account of the giving of the law at Mount Sinai extends from Exod 20 through Num 10. They then depart for the land of promise but then must wander in the wilderness for forty years. As they finally get to the brink of crossing the Jordan river, they stop, and Moses gives a speech the size of Deuteronomy! Moses here recalls the major events of Israel's history, repeats many of the legal instructions already delivered, and gives a series of reiterated warnings about obedience in the land.

If you were a reader expecting "one unified story about Jesus," at this point you may decide you've taken a wrong turn somewhere. Who is Israel? Where is Jesus? How long is this story anyway? Knowing that the NT is coming, in the middle of Leviticus you might have echoed my kids' favorite car ride question, "Are we there yet?"

If the Bible is a story, it's certainly not one like a novel that unfolds chapter by chapter with a continuous sequence. The Bible's story starts and stops, doubles back, repeats, rehearses, anticipates a later time, speeds up over events that seem pretty important, and then slows way down around details that don't seem to matter!

* * *

As we keep moving, we encounter many more complicating factors. The book of Joshua covers a single leader's lifetime, but the book of Judges covers around 400 years! The main storyline continues with Samuel and the first kings Saul, David, and Solomon. But then the story starts jumping back and forth from the Northern Kingdom to the Southern Kingdom in the book of Kings. This book also ends on a bit of a depressing cliff-hanger with the disaster of Israel in exile in a foreign land. The books of Ezra and Nehemiah tell of the slow and halting return of the people to Israel, but the book of Chronicles starts with Adam (1 Chron 1:1), mentions the time after the exile (1 Chron 9), and then backs up to the reign of David before eventually coming to an end right before the people get to return to the land.

As a reader expecting the story to continue, you are likely surprised that there are no more big narrative books in the OT. You encounter poetic and prophetic books that don't tell the next part of the story but rather are commenting on parts of the story you've already encountered! Isaiah sees the Lord fill the temple in the year that king Uzziah died. Ezekiel receives a vision by the rivers of Babylon. Jeremiah warns of coming destruction and then witnesses the fall of Israel. The writer of Lamentations languishes in lament over a destroyed Jerusalem. Ruth survives in the time of the Judges; Job suffers in the era of Abraham; Daniel shows up in Babylon; and Esther is in the courts of Persia.

The wide-ranging scope of many OT books is highlighted especially in the book of Psalms. This book includes a psalm of Moses, psalms of David and Solomon, and also psalms that speak of return from exile. This collection thus covers the entirety of the nation of Israel's history!

* * *

Back to your reading plan, you've made your way to the NT. Finally! Now we can get to the one story that speaks of Christ. This expectation goes smoothly as you read Matthew's Gospel. After the post-resurrection great commission of Jesus at the end of the narrative, though, you might reasonably expect to hear about what happens next. You're ready to see the disciples make disciples of all nations!

The last words of Matthew spoke of the "end of the age" (Matt 28:20), but as you turn the page to Mark, you encounter a book about "the beginning of the gospel of Jesus Christ" (Mk 1:1). We're starting over again! In the third Gospel, Luke roots his narrative in the testimony of those who were there "from the beginning" of Jesus's life and ministry. John even begins his Gospel in the beginning of all things! Even here at the apex of the biblical canon, we still don't get one story about Christ; we get four!

If you've ever picked up a chronological study Bible (one that aims to put the biblical books "in chronological order"), you can helpfully see that it's actually impossible to put the biblical books in chronological order. You have to break up books and splice them together with bits and larger sections of other books.

We can certainly affirm the authoritative truthfulness of each of these biblical books. But a close reading of the Bible as a whole should also shape our expectations about what we're reading. Our assessment needs to be able to handle four overlapping yet distinct books that cover the same ground. It needs to be able to account for a story of the early churches that suddenly stops with Paul in prison in Rome and only continues in a vision of the end of days with John on the island of Patmos!

We need to specify *what kind of story* the Bible tells. If we're expecting a single narrative stream that progresses in a one-chapter-right-after-the-next sequence, we are likely to be confused and bewildered when we actually do the hard work of reading the Bible! This mismatched expectation is oftentimes the reason someone stops their Bible reading plan and returns to a different mode of Bible intake (perhaps a devotional or a verse-a-day format). How many Bible-in-a-year resolutions have run aground on the submerged reef of tabernacle instructions or have hit the hidden sandbar of census details or lists of land distribution?

In light of this diversity, is it even proper to speak of a unified story that the Bible tells? Recognizing the diversity of biblical books and the nature of biblical narratives give us a good starting point for conceiving of the Bible's grand story in a way that resonates with the approach to biblical theology we're developing.

One of the hopes of biblical theology is that the careful study of the whole Bible on its own terms will give us the training that will help us persevere in our reading. Doing some of the heavy lifting of considering the "big picture" of biblical books, collections, and the canon as a whole can give us the muscle memory that we need when we encounter verses, chapters, scenes, and concepts that are unexpected or seemingly out of sequence.

In this chapter and the next, we will explore the ways that it is true that the Bible tells one grand story that gives us eternal truth and the knowledge of God's will. Using a template we've already mentioned before, the question here is not *that* the Bible tells a story, but *how* the Bible tells its story. The Scriptures tell one story that speaks of Christ, but we need to train our ears to discern and appreciate the diverging melody lines that harmonize in this grand symphony.

To begin, I suggest that the following categories can help us argue for the coherence of the Bible's message from beginning to end: the many narratives, the mega-narrative, and the meta-narrative of the Bible. Even if they go unacknowledged, each of these areas is usually a component of how we typically talk about the story that the Bible tells.

The Many Narratives (the Stories)

One of the most basic reasons why the category of "story" is appropriate when thinking about the "big picture" of the Bible is the considerable quantity of biblical literature that tells some sort of story (over two-thirds of the Bible!). Indeed, any biblical reader will immediately encounter a disproportionately large portion of narrative texts.

The Bible is a book brimming with narrative. In this respect, a majority of biblical texts are either narratives or directly connected to narrative sections that influence the setting and interpretation of those non-narrative portions. The predominance of narrative in the biblical collection has a profound effect on the shape of the collection as a whole.

One of the immediately noticeable features of biblical narratives is that they are realistic historical narratives. This genre choice made by the biblical authors entails that one of the most prominent things the Bible does is tell stories. During most of your time reading the Bible, you will experience some sort of story.

Sometimes the story is cosmic, like when God speaks the world into existence in Gen 1. Sometimes the story is mundane, like when the tabernacle designs are delivered in Exod 26. Sometimes the story is dramatic, like when Paul proclaims the gospel as a prisoner during a shipwreck on his journey to see the emperor in Rome (Acts 27). Sometimes the story is relatively static, like when Paul preaches under house arrest after he finally arrives in Rome (Acts 28).

The many narratives found throughout the Bible come in all different shapes and sizes, with different theological purposes and textual strategies. Nevertheless, every major grouping within the biblical canon includes significant segments of narrative. This scenario must be reckoned with as we consider the Bible's overarching shape. In this regard, a focus on the storyline of Scripture in biblical theology is an emphasis that follows directly from the sheer number of narratives in the biblical collection.

The Mega-Narrative (the Grand Storyline)

A closely related reason for emphasizing story when thinking about the message of the Bible as a whole is not just the *amount* of stories but also their textual *interconnections*.

Because the biblical writers often composed their books in light of other biblical narratives (especially the book of Moses), a basic coherence in worldview and theological framework runs through the biblical texts. When gathered together into a collection, the *many* biblical narratives generate an overarching *mega*-narrative that begins in Genesis and ends in Revelation.

Directly related to the Genesis-to-Revelation storyline that biblical theology seeks to capture, there is also a series of thematic and intertextual connections between Gen 1–3 and Rev 21–22. The first and last chapters of the grand storyline of the biblical canon furnish bookends for what God is doing in the world. In the beginning, God creates the heavens and the earth. In the end, he creates a new heaven and a new earth.

Biblical authors across both testaments set their history of redemption within this biblical-theological framework. The task of the biblical theologian is to highlight the way each textual part contributes to this storied whole. The shape of the narratives found within the biblical canon is sufficient to produce a grand narrative storyline or mega-narrative that situates readers as they travel through each literary corpus and from one grouping to the next within the larger collection.

This hermeneutical reading strategy arises from the fact that these many biblical narratives have been gathered together in just this way and have been associated with one another within the context of a canonical collection.

This location within a collection not only enables readers to perceive the connections between books but also allows them to see each book as part of the grand narrative storyline that spans the two-testament collection.

The Meta-Narrative
(the Story That Explains All Other Stories)

As noted above, because of the biblical canon, the many narratives of the Bible contribute to a kind of mega-narrative. This grand storyline, in turn, generates a series of assumptions about who God is, who we are, and how we are to respond as a result. In other words, the mega-narrative collectively generates a *meta*-narrative.

A meta-narrative is a kind of commentary on the function of the larger narrative itself. The meta-narrative includes a series of claims about the nature of reality that are implied or required by the many narratives and the biblical mega-narrative. The Bible's meta-narrative is also related to what is often called a "Christian worldview." How does believing the testimony of the Scriptures shape and inform your view of the world?

The biblical texts individually and collectively make claims upon their readers. The biblical narratives claim not only that "all the world's a stage" but also that all the world is on *its* stage!

The stories recounted in the biblical canon encourage a certain view of the world, one in which readers are implicated as part of the "real world" those narratives generate.[1]

The meaning of biblical texts and the comprehensive message of the biblical mega-narrative put pressure on us as readers to view the world in a certain way. For someone who *reads* and also *heeds* the grand storyline of the Bible, the most pressing worldview questions have textually rooted answers.

Who am I? What am I? Why am I here? Why is there something rather than nothing? What has gone wrong in the world? How will this all end? Believers have answers to these existential questions because they accept the meaning of a storyline that is all-encompassing.

Those of us familiar with the riches of Scripture sometimes underestimate the theological horizon that is opened up by even briefly stated biblical sentences. "In the beginning, God created the heavens and the earth." This is the kind of truth that rearranges one's mental architecture. It doesn't just adjust someone's lens prescription; it enables the ability to see.

While these terms are often used loosely or interchangeably, it is also helpful to observe the distinctions we've discussed here. The biblical texts are one thing (the many narratives), the way they relate to one another within the biblical canon is another (the mega-narrative), and the set of assumptions we affirm when we accept the truth of this grand storyline is yet another (the meta-narrative).

Canonical Complexity and Coherence

In order to do justice to the special revelation we have received in the Scriptures, we need to affirm both the canonical *complexity* and *coherence* of the grand storyline of the Bible. The context of the biblical canon is what allows us to access and understand the overarching biblical mega-narrative. The Biblical canon includes individual books with discrete messages placed and arranged within a broader collection that communicates that they are in some way unified.

A community of readers will still have to grapple with what that unity and diversity entails (and thus the practice of biblical theology is perennial!), but it is just this task that is required of anyone who seeks to mine the treasures of the Christian Scriptures.

The many narratives of the Bible do not unfold and intersect like a single piece of cloth. Rather they form an overarching storyline when woven together within the same collection. This textual tapestry is more like a lovingly crafted quilt than a quickly manufactured bedsheet.[2]

The narrative storyline that emerges is coherent but also complex. The big story of the Bible begins and then reaches its final destination, but it doesn't always take the same route or move in a straight line.

As Dempster observes, "The larger Story is not one-dimensional. And although the Bible is a coherent Story, it is a sprawling one, a sort of ramshackle narrative with many stops and starts, dead ends and detours, and any number of high and low points. Often it is only the perspective gained from a later point in the story that enables one to see the overall shape of the narrative."[3]

The end goal of biblical theology at this point is not to flatten out these contours but rather to make sense of the textual topography that the biblical mega-narrative lays out before us within the scope of the biblical canon.

Conclusion

To sum up the big idea of this chapter: In the study of biblical theology, it is helpful to keep in mind the relationship between the many narratives of the Bible, the way these narratives intersect within the canonical collection to form a grand storyline (the mega-narrative), and the worldview this storyline assumes and pressures readers to adopt (the meta-narrative).

In other words, the canonical sequence of biblical stories is part of a comprehensive storyline that claims to be the story that explains all other stories!

These categories can help us grapple with the way that the Bible *is* and *is not* a "story."

There is a canonical *complexity* to our sacred text, but there is also a canonical *coherence* that has the divinely granted function of shaping our entire view of the world.

Discussion & Reflection

1. This chapter argued that in some ways the Bible *is* a story and in other ways it is *not*. Why would it be important to recognize both of these dimensions?

2. If you've ever tried to read through the entire Bible from beginning to end, what did you find was most challenging and most rewarding about this reading journey? Where or when was it the hardest to keep going? How could the notion of a "grand storyline" help you out along the way?

3. There are many biblical statements that affect and immediately shape our view of the world. If you believe that these texts are true, then it also means that other theological realities are true. The example given above is Gen 1:1. Discuss some of the theological affirmations you have to make in order to believe these texts: Ps 23:1; Nah 1:7; Jn 3:16; Jn 16:33.

Notes:

1. Cf. Auerbach's classic observation about the way biblical narrative functions differently than other ancient literature: "The Bible's claim to truth is not only far more urgent than Homer's, it is tyrannical—it excludes all other claims. The world of the Scripture stories is not satisfied with claiming to be a historically true reality—it insists that it is the only real world, is destined for autocracy." See *Mimesis*, 14–15. Auerbach concludes his point by noting that "the Scripture stories do not, like Homer's, court our favor, they do not flatter us that they may please us and enchant us—they seek to subject us, and if we refuse to be subjected, we are rebels" (15). Vanhoozer also notes that "to read the Bible is to enter into its world, at least momentarily, a world dominated by the word of God that addresses us, and by the God who awaits our response" (*Mere Christian Hermeneutics*, 16).
2. Sailhamer uses a similar analogy to illustrate the nature of composition in *How We Got the Bible*, 37.
3. As quoted in Spellman, *Invitation to BT*, 61. Cf. Dempster, *Return of the Kingdom*, 10: "That pathway marked through the Bible is not straight ahead but more like a long winding road that goes forward, curving off to the side, tracking backward, zigzagging in another direction before advancing again."

4

Recognizing Canonical Signposts
Guidance for Traversing the Bible's Literary Landscape

After considering some of the central categories that allow us to grasp the sweep of the Bible's narratives, we can also note some of the major patterns that show up across the biblical canon that help us make sense of this sometimes sprawling storyline. Though there are many patterns we could mention, here we'll focus on strategic summaries of Israel's history, accounts of the biblical covenants, and the network of the Bible's central themes.

1. Remembering and Repeating the Biblical Storyline

The narratives found in the biblical canon not only *narrate* the events they recount, but also *interpret* them. Biblical narratives are a combination of story and significance, of text and event, of revelatory deeds and revelatory words. Within these narrative books, theological arguments are made by the authors about God's person and character.

For the purpose of biblical theology, it is particularly significant that there are many biblical narratives, that they have been strategically collected, and that they narrate and interpret God's work in the world. At distinctive points in the narrative flow of the OT and NT collections, there are reflective summaries of redemptive history. These notable passages demonstrate that later biblical writers understood their past not only in light of an oral history, but also in light of specific accounts found in previously written biblical texts.

When a later prophet recounts the exodus, for example, his portrayal often echoes the literary presentation of this event found in the book of Exodus (e.g., Isa 43:16–21). Even within the Pentateuch itself, there are several accounts of a single event that build upon and interpret one another. To give one example, Exod 19–24 describes the giving of the Ten Commandments (or "ten words") and the book of the covenant. In Deut 5, this scene and these words are reiterated and interpreted for a new generation of Israelites. So, even within the same biblical book, events that are initially narrated become subsequently recounted and interpreted.

This pattern of narration and interpretation is a notable aspect of narratives in general and an especially crucial feature to observe regarding the biblical narratives in particular.[1] As you make use of the biblical storyline in the study of biblical theology, it is imperative to take this textual and authorial feature into account.

The biblical authors have already sought to present and interpret the meaning and significance of redemptive history for future generations of readers. As members of that group of future readers, our primary task is to discern what the biblical authors have given to us in their texts. These interpretive summaries of redemptive history can inform the way we summarize and interpret that same redemptive history. In this way, the biblical writers provide guidance for biblical readers in understanding the nature and significance of the overarching storyline of the biblical narratives.

In particular, as you make your way through the grand storyline of the Bible, you should make special note of the final speeches given by major figures at the end of their lives.

These "famous last words" often include a summary of redemptive history, interpretation of God's past actions, commentary on the people's covenant relationship, and a word of exhortation for a future generation.

- Last words of Jacob (Gen 49)

- Last words of Moses (Deut 27–33)

- Last words of Joshua (Josh 23–24)

- Last words of Samuel (1 Sam 12–13)

- Last words of David (2 Sam 22–23; 1 Kgs 2)

- Last words of the author of Kings (2 Kgs 17 and 25)

- Last words of Stephen (Acts 6–7)

- Last words of Paul (Acts 20 and 28)

- Last words of Jesus (Matt 28; Luke 24; Acts 1; Rev 22)

There are many speeches in the narratives of the storyline that are important, but the speeches listed above are particularly significant in their narration and interpretation of redemptive history as it unfolds across the biblical canon.

For example, Jacob's last words include blessings for each of his sons (which recalls important points in the previous narratives) but also have an orientation toward the future (Jacob prefaces his speech by mentioning the "end of days,"

Gen 49:1). At the end of his life and at the close of his book, Moses lists these same names but now in reference to the tribes they have become in the nation of Israel (Deut 32–33).

These textual connections help tie the story of the book of Moses together, but Moses's final words here also prophetically anticipate the broad outline of Israel's future. Moses reminds the people to remain faithful when they enter the land of promise, warns against rejecting God's instructions, and then predicts that they will in fact turn away from the Lord and be taken away from the land. While they are in that land of exile, if they return to the Lord in faith and repentance, the Lord will bring them back and establish them once again as his people in the land of promise (Deut 29–30).

Remarkably, the prophetic history that comes next in Joshua, Judges, Samuel, and Kings follows the broad outlines of Moses's prophetic portrayal. In fact, the "last words" of the narrator of Kings echo the language and substance of Moses's speech when he gives a theological interpretation of Israel's destruction and descent into exile (2 Kgs 17). The people had broken the covenant expectations and neglected proper worship "until the Lord removed Israel out of his sight, as he had spoken by all his servants the prophets" (2 Kgs 17:23).

These kinds of textual links help us see the interconnection of these important passages, but they also provide guidance for us as we try to get a handle on the long history of Israel. In presenting these "famous last words" at these pivotal turning points in Israel's history, the biblical authors are giving us a biblical-theological map to orient us to the inner workings of God's work in the world.

2. Recognizing the Significance of Biblical Covenants

The grand storyline of the Bible, supplied by the canonical context, tells a consistent and coherent story of God's purposes in the world and among his people. Recognizing this small-scale and large-scale textual feature of the biblical canon, we can ask: Is there anything that helps characterize the focus of the many narratives of the Bible, the mega-narrative of the Bible, and the patterns that make up the meta-narrative of the Bible?

Indeed there is! A prominent and recurring thread that runs throughout the story of the Scriptures is the story of the covenants. The biblical covenants are major signposts in the story that the Scriptures tell.

But why select the covenants for special attention within the flow of redemptive history? Why should we spend more time directly considering the biblical covenants? The answer to this question draws upon the previously established points about the nature of narrative. As readers, we focus on the major covenants in the biblical storyline because the biblical authors themselves focused on the biblical covenants as they composed and shaped how the biblical storyline was presented in their texts and in their books.

In fact, the only reason biblical readers are able to detect the strategic importance of the covenants for God's purposes in the world is because of the strategic role they play in biblical texts. The biblical authors "slow down" redemptive history at just these points and provide both a narration and interpretation of the establishment of these covenant relationships at just these moments in redemptive history at just these textual locations.

When we focus on the covenants, the story they tell, and the implications they inevitably bear for the nature of God and his purposes in the world, we are seeking to follow the lead of the biblical authors themselves.

What is a biblical covenant? We can define a covenant here simply and broadly as *a relationship based on a promise.*[2] More specifically, a biblical covenant is a relationship in the biblical storyline between God and a group of his created people that is based on a spoken promise. These covenant relationships usually include the formal expectation of blessings for obedience and curses for disobedience.

As you make your way through the grand storyline of the Bible, you will encounter six major covenants or covenant relationships.

- Covenant with **Adam**
  (Gen 1–3, esp. 1:26–31; 2:15–17)

- Covenant with **Noah**
  (Gen 6–9, esp. 8:20–9:17)

- Covenant with **Abraham**
  (Gen 12–22, esp. 12:1–7; 15:1–21)

- Covenant with **Moses** and Israel
  (Exod 19–24)

- Covenant with **David**
  (2 Sam 7, esp. 7:8–17; 1 Chron 17)

- The **New** Covenant
  (Deut 30:6–10; Jer 31:31–35; Ezek 36:22–32; Heb 8–10)

The biblical covenants can provide a theological framework that affects and enhances your reading of Scripture. When you read a given passage of Scripture, you can ask, "What biblical covenant is in the foreground of this text?" Additionally, you can ask, "Is there a biblical covenant in the background of this text that elucidates its broader context?" Asking these questions will help you understand where the passage you are studying fits in the larger storyline of God's redemptive purposes.

Because of these textual and theological features, the covenants are signposts that direct readers through sections of the biblical canon and also portions of the Bible's grand storyline. They also direct readers to focus on the all-important relationship between God and his people. Oftentimes, a biblical writer will appeal to one or more of these covenants in order to communicate his message.

For example, in prophetic literature the prophets frequently use elements of the Mosaic covenant, the Davidic covenant, and the new covenant to convey their message. The prophets set up the idea of the need for complete obedience to the Lord. To drive home their emphasis upon the need for repentance and obedience, the prophets often keep the Mosaic covenant and its stipulations in the foreground.

However, the fact of the matter is that the people do not obey these stipulations. Consequently, the prophets appeal to the hope of the Davidic covenant in the background. As the situation worsens through the sustained lack of repentance and obedience, the prophets use the failure of the Mosaic covenant (due to the people's lack of faith) to point to the need for the new covenant, the measure of hope. This particular sequence captures the thematic trajectory of several prophetic books.

For the NT writers, the biblical covenants are the means by which they tell the story of Jesus as the Christ. For instance, the very first words of the NT signal that the gospel requires knowing the covenants. Matthew begins, "The book of the genealogy of Jesus Christ, son of David, son of Abraham" (Matt 1:1).

Jesus's identity as the promised messiah is deepened by reference to biblical covenants and so is his work of atonement. During the first Lord's Supper when Jesus says, "this cup that is poured out for you is the new covenant in my blood" (Lk 22:20; cf. 1 Cor 11:25), it is no wonder that mention of the forgiveness of sins follows, because one of the promises of the new covenant is the forgiveness of sins (Matt 26:28; Jer 31:31–34).

When reading the OT and NT, the "story of the Bible" is often a way of speaking about the "story of the covenants." The way the covenants build upon one another also implies an important sense of progression and development as readers make their way through the biblical collection from beginning to end.

Knowing the biblical covenants themselves, the narratives that portray them, and the story they are connected to will equip you to find your way in the Word and in the world.

Keep your eyes on the covenants and you will gain a line of sight into who God is and what God does.

3. Tracing the Network of Central Themes

Another important aspect of biblical literature that biblical theology highlights is the collection of central themes that show up and develop across the biblical canon. While recognizing that anything that appears in biblical literature is important and worthy of further study, there are nevertheless certain themes that are especially strategic and pervasive. These themes enable us to see interconnections between the Law, the Prophets, the Writings, the Gospels, Acts, the Letters, and Revelation.

When a theme shows up in a strategic or pervasive way in each of these groupings, we can confidently classify it as a central theme. In other words, this type of theme is central to the message and textual intention of the biblical authors who have written their books with specific purposes in mind.

These themes help us as readers to recognize what merits the greatest amount of attention in the Scriptures. The goal of this type of study is to explore the development of these themes across the canon and observe how each theme progresses at different points in the grand storyline of the Bible.

Rather than pinpoint a single center to organize the produce of biblical theology, the more fruitful way forward is to articulate a collection of central biblical-theological themes that capture major swaths of the theological message found across the Bible.

In the end, a collection of themes better captures what we find within a collection of diverse yet unified biblical writings. Within the framework of the canon, the covenants, and the Christ, we find several central themes that the biblical authors themselves introduce and develop.[3] This window into the shape and analysis of the Bible highlights the remarkable level of coherence that the biblical canon possesses as a collection on its own terms.

Some of the central themes that have been noted by readers throughout church history include:

- God's glory seen as the basis of all of God's acts from creation to redemption

- God's covenant relationship that he establishes with his people

- God's presence experienced in divinely established places such as the garden, the tabernacle, the temple, and the new Jerusalem

- The relationship between the creation of the world in the beginning and the creation of a new heavens and a new earth in the end

- The way that the theme of redemption intersects with the theological concepts of sacrifice, atonement, and reconciliation

- How the person and work of Christ relate to the prophetic portrayal of the coming Messiah and the Day of the Lord

Most of the time, a "central theme" is developed in concert with other central themes or a network of smaller themes or "sub-themes." Each of these central themes and the web of theological trajectories that either feed into or flow out from them are some of the most productive and exciting threads that tie the storyline of the Bible together.

Sometimes a theme will appear so frequently that its importance is clear even though we still need to think carefully about it. For example, the giving and function of the law (the Mosaic covenant and its legal stipulations) is an obviously important theme to grapple with as we read through the OT and the NT. Half of the book of Exodus, the entirety of Leviticus, a good deal of Numbers, and the main argument of Deuteronomy give a narrative account of the giving of the law, several collections of the actual legislation that accompanies the national covenant, as well as an *interpretation* of the law itself.

Much of the following narrative shows the blessings that come from obedience to God's law and the bitter consequences of rejecting this covenant. Jesus spoke about fulfilling the law, he debated the Jewish leadership about it, and several NT epistles grapple with the meaning and status of the law in the new covenant community (e.g., significant portions of Romans, Galatians, Hebrews, and James!).

A biblical theology of "the law" will need to take each of these contexts into account alongside the development that takes place throughout the canonical collection.

Other times a theme might be mentioned only a handful of times and yet be significant enough to be considered a "central theme." For instance, the phrase "image of God" only shows up in a few places in the Bible, but the notion that human beings have inherent worth and dignity because they are created by God and bear his image undergirds the whole of Christian ethics and informs much of what we say about both humanity and the Christian life.

In a biblical theology of "the image of God," we might point out that the first instance of this theme is in one of the most prominent places in the biblical canon: the beginning of all things in the creation account of Genesis. It's also spoken by God himself as part of the divine speech that brings the world into existence.

We might also note that the two follow-up reiterations of humanity created in the image of God occur at strategic points in the early storyline of Genesis (after the fall into sin in Gen 5:1–2 and after the judgment of the flood in Gen 9:6–7).

More broadly, we would also be able to reflect on the continued use of this theme in relation to the Christian life (Col 3:9–10; Jas 3:9) as well as what it means for Christ to be the "image of the invisible God" (Col 1:15; 2 Cor 4:4; Heb 1:3).

Of course, all of these connections will require careful thinking and theological reasoning. However, when we consider the patterns we've explored in this chapter, we're grappling with passages, theological concepts, and thematic threads that the biblical authors themselves have placed before our eyes as readers.

Strategic summary statements, accounts of the biblical covenants, and the development of central themes each provide guidance for us as we make our way through the Bible's storyline and reflect upon the meaning of biblical books.

Discussion & Reflection:

1. The "famous last words" of many prominent biblical figures often give us guidance for the major developments of the broader story of redemption. Take a look at Jesus's last words in Luke's Gospel (Lk 24:36–49). How does this final speech sum up Luke's narrative and anticipate what comes next in the book of Acts?

2. How does the story of the biblical covenants help us discern and reflect upon the heart of the grand storyline of the Bible? How are the covenants like "signposts" for us as we read?

3. Using the categories of these last two chapters, reflect on the way the opening of Matthew's Gospel (Matt 1:1–25) connects the story of Jesus to the story of the covenants. Do you see any of the central themes of the OT mentioned here? Some of these mentions are direct and obvious; others are indirect or more subtly implied. How does seeing these connections deepen your appreciation for what Matthew is communicating here in the first words of the NT?

Notes:

1. Significant examples of a biblical figure or writer recounting Israel's history in light of its previous portrayal in Israel's Scriptures include Neh 9:5–37; Ps 78; Pss 105–106; and Heb 11. For a close reading of many of these types of textual examples, see Shepherd, *Textual World*, 5–86. Shepherd identifies biblical-theological summaries from the Law (Deut 6:20–25; 11:1–17; 26:5–9), the Prophets (Josh 24:1–15; Judg 2:1–5; 6:7–10; 10:11–16; 1 Sam 12:6–17; Jer 2:1–13; Ezek 20; Amos 2:6–3:2; Mic 6:1–8), the Writings (Pss 78; 105–106; 135–36; Neh 9), and the NT (Acts 7; 13:13–41; Heb 11). Though these passages have often been understood in terms of tradition history or "salvation history," Shepherd argues that these texts present themselves as exegetical in nature. On this textual feature, see also Bruno, Compton, and McFadden, *BT According to the Apostles: How the Earliest Christians told the Story of Israel* (IVP, 2020).

2. This phrasing is a working definition designed to provide a starting point for readers as they approach these strategic points in the biblical storyline and in strategic textual locations in the biblical canon. There are a great many scholarly discussions (and debates!) about the concept of "covenant" in the Bible and in the ancient world. The point we're making here about the covenants could fit within several of the broader theological systems that emphasize covenants (for more on this discussion, see Spellman, *Invitation to Biblical Theology*, 65–68).

3. For a development of this framework of "the canon, the covenants, and the Christ" (along with the three major sections of this chapter), see chapter 2 of Spellman, *Invitation to BT*.

5

The Gospel of This Grand Storyline
The Depth & Dimensions of the Bible's Good News

Now that we have discussed some of the ways that the Bible holds together, we can start thinking about some of the core features of its message. One of the exciting aspects of biblical theology is that many of the patterns and themes that help us see how the Bible fits together are the same ones that show us the depth and dimensions of the Bible's "good news."

The NT authors proclaim the gospel of our Lord Jesus Christ. Paying attention to what they pay attention to will help us see the profound depth of Christianity. A close examination of the teaching *of* Jesus and the proclamation *about* Jesus reveals a strong connection between the meaning of biblical texts and the message of the gospel.

The Gospel as a Story That Takes Two Testaments to Tell

In several theologically significant NT passages, the proclamation of the gospel is connected to the biblical-theological tools that we've already mentioned. In particular, an exploration of the richness of the gospel message is also an opportunity to consider the relationship between the OT and the NT. These texts draw together the shape of the canonical collection, the unfolding narrative storyline of redemptive history, and the central theme of God's saving activity in Jesus Christ.

In other words, the biblical authors themselves teach their readers that the gospel is a story that takes two testaments to tell.[1]

The Preached Word and the Remembered Christ

The prevalent and profound use of OT Scripture is a well-established feature of virtually every text in the NT. The portrayal and proclamation of the gospel message thus occurs in this intertextual atmosphere. A central task of NT theology is to articulate the meaning and function of the apostolic kerygma (the "preached word" of the apostles).[2]

The preaching of the apostles structures the way that readers of the NT understand its overall message and receive its most significant claims. For our purpose, it is critical to observe that the *apostolic* kerygma was an *intertextual* kerygma from its inception. The portrayal of apostolic preaching in NT narratives and the content of apostolic teaching in NT epistles supports this foundational characterization of the kerygma of the earliest churches.

In the opening sermon in the book of Acts, Peter explains the presence of the Holy Spirit as an indication that the "last days" of God's plan of redemption had dawned on the basis of the work of the incarnate Christ (Acts 2:14–41). In order to demonstrate this new covenant reality, Peter quotes and reflects upon texts from the book of Joel and several psalms of David.[3]

In his next major address, Peter returns to an account of the crucifixion and resurrection of Jesus and asserts that the suffering of the Messiah is the fulfillment of what God had "predicted through all the prophets" (CSB, Acts 2:18). He then cites the expectation of a coming prophet like Moses (2:22–23; cf. Deut 18:15–19) and the prior promise of the Abrahamic covenant (2:25; cf. Gen 12:3).

Paul also follows this pattern of proclamation in his preaching about Jesus as the Christ. When asked to give a "word of exhortation" in the synagogue at Antioch of Pisidia after the reading of "the Law and the Prophets" (Acts 13:13–41), Paul recounts key moments from Israel's history with a special focus on the Davidic covenant. He identifies Jesus as this expected son of David, summarizes Jesus's death and resurrection, and calls for a believing response. In this sermon, too, he quotes from strategic Davidic psalms and prophetic passages about the Messiah, the meaning of the mosaic covenant, and the "good news of the promise" that is recounted in the Scriptures.[4]

In addition to this narrative portrayal, the letters of the NT also reveal the intertextual threads woven into the fabric of the apostolic kerygma. In the opening of his letter to the Romans, Paul speaks of the "gospel of God" as a message about Jesus that was "promised beforehand through his prophets in the Holy Scriptures" (Rom 1:2). Paul identifies Jesus as the Christ by noting that in the incarnation Jesus was a descendant of David and has been raised from the dead (Rom 1:3–4).

In the closing chapters of his first letter to the Corinthians, Paul gives a memorable expression of the gospel that he received and passes on to others: "That Christ died for our sins according to the Scriptures, that he was buried, that he was raised on the third day according to the Scriptures" (1 Cor 15:3–4). What is particularly noteworthy for our purpose here is that in what is perhaps the earliest expression of the essential gospel message, written texts are already functioning as the anchoring location of new covenant revelation about Jesus and the salvation he has secured.

In his second letter to Timothy, Paul envisions the process of passing along this preached message of the gospel. "What you have heard from me in the presence of many witnesses," he tells Timothy, "commit to faithful men who will be able to teach others also" (2 Tim 2:2). After outlining this process of discipleship, Paul also indicates the content of this proclaimed message. He urges, "Remember Jesus Christ, risen from the dead and descended from David, for which I suffer to the point of being bound like a criminal. But the word of God is not bound" (2 Tim 2:8–9).

Each of the terms in this brief sequence in 2 Tim 2:8 points to textual treasure chests that can fund our theological reflection. When NT authors mention the title Christ, they virtually always connect it to a strategic text or concept from the OT. In this formulation, when Paul urges, "Remember Jesus Christ," he immediately adds, "descendant of David." When the prophets call their readers to repentance and remind them of future hope, they often hold out a vision of a coming descendant of David who would one day arrive and make all things right again.

In this way, Paul is providing a Bible-length, life-long guide for reflecting on the theological significance of the person and work of Jesus. The gospel that Paul proclaims requires a further phrase, namely, "risen from the dead." Here, the promise of the OT is joined by the proclamation of the NT witness. Every element of this sentence is like a hyperlink that you can click to open an entire web of biblical-theological truth. In these phrases, Paul provides a bite-sized whole-Bible biblical theology:

Jesus (NT), the Christ (OT), descendent of David (OT), risen from the dead (NT).

Paul also adds that these descriptions are "according to his gospel" (2 Tim 2:9). In other words, the confession and contemplation of Jesus as the resurrected son of David was at the burning core of his gospel preaching. When Paul speaks of the gospel, the good news, he has in mind the message that he constantly proclaims.

In order for Paul to be a *proclaimer of the gospel*, he must also be a *reader of the Scriptures*.

These passages from Acts and the NT epistles provide a snapshot of the apostolic preaching which proclaimed Christ through extensive reflection on the history of redemption and strategic texts from across the Law, the Prophets, and the Psalms. Passages like these draw together the NT preaching of the apostles and the OT promises of the prophets.

While there are many other literary and theological aspects of the passages discussed in this section, one thematic thread that emerges is the way the preached gospel is interwoven with the exposition of individual biblical texts, explained with reference to canonical sub-collections, and embedded within the unfolding storyline of redemptive history. These textual features provide warrant for the theological assertion that the gospel is a story that takes two testaments to tell.

Gospel Pathways through the Canonical Mountain Ranges

Alongside the articulation and portrayal of the apostolic preaching, the Gospel narratives also recount Jesus's own messianic interpretation of his death and resurrection.

The Gospel writers have also composed their narratives in light of this teaching that they initially received from Jesus himself.

Briefly considering the opening of the first Gospel can allow us to continue our reflection of the gospel message and can also provide a deeper orientation to the relationship between the testaments.

At the center of the task of biblical theology is reckoning with and reflecting upon the relationship between the OT and the NT. There is a host of interpretive issues that must be addressed when tackling this question (e.g., the difference between the text & ordering of the Greek translations and the Hebrew editions).

Even so, considering this topic at this point in our study can bear much fruit. One of the reasons for this is because how you conceptualize the relationship and dynamic between the testaments will shape how you will understand the message of the Bible as a whole and the reading of many biblical texts in particular.

How you understand the way the OT relates to the NT will profoundly affect your understanding of the gospel message Jesus and the apostles proclaim.

Avoiding a Few Roadblocks: An Unfortunate Tendency and a Common Mistake

1. *Functional Neglect of the OT.* Before we work through a few helpful categories for this task, it's worth briefly examining a few wrong turns. One unhelpful but unfortunately common tendency is to view the OT as optional or basic background information for the NT. In this perspective, the primary function of the OT is to provide a supplemental historical context for the story and message of the NT. Sometimes this viewpoint is explicitly stated and argued for. Other times it simply operates as an unstated assumption that affects the way whole-Bible reading is done.

Among those with a high view of Scripture, this basic construal usually shows up as simple neglect of the OT as a coherent collection on par with the NT. A preacher might spend years on Romans with only a few OT interludes in the Psalms. Or, the OT might be emphasized only when the NT directly references one of its narrative figures or prominent passages. This functional neglect of the OT as a whole tends to imply that the OT needs to be known but not studied in depth nor mined for theological meaning in the same way that the NT is pursued.

2. *Adopting a Singular & Totalizing Rubric for the Relationship between the Testaments.* In addition to basic neglect of the OT, one further mistake that might be made is to adopt a single rubric for understanding the relationship between the testaments. In this scenario, a particular characterization is the dominant way one connects the OT and the NT to the virtual exclusion of other possibilities.

Of course, most readers or interpretive traditions will gravitate toward one or another category for a variety of important and legitimate reasons (e.g., whether emphasis is placed on continuity or discontinuity between the biblical covenants).

Each of the major ways of characterizing the relationship between the testaments, though, has unique strengths and limitations. Exploring these strengths and limitations will serve you well as you reflect upon the shape of the two-testament witness of the Christian canon.

The Opening of Matthew as a Roadmap to Canonical Connections

While these provide a strong enough reason to employ and examine multiple concepts, there is a further motivation that is expressly exegetical. In strategic fashion, the biblical authors utilize several complementary ways of drawing upon the OT Scriptures. The theologically informed exegetical moves that the biblical authors make can teach us some of the best ways to connect the writings of the prophets and the writings of the apostles.

In addition to its function as the first entry in a fourfold Gospel grouping that begins the NT as a whole, the book of Matthew also explicitly signals to its readers that the OT Scriptures are integral to the meaning of the gospel story.

In Matt 1–4, we can see several major categories for relating the testaments working in harmony with one another. There is of course much we could say about each of these passages, but here I will simply point out a few elements that are relevant for our current discussion.

1. *The Grand Storyline of Redemptive History:* A striking feature of Matthew's Gospel is the way it delays any narrative action until after a relatively extensive rehearsal of Israel's history. The story begins in Matt 1:18 where the narrator notes, "Now the birth of Jesus Christ took place in this way."

The entire section of 1:1–17 is non-narrative details that make reference in some way to a dimension of Israel's history. What's more, the opening line makes clear that both history and theology are in view. Matthew begins, "The book of the genealogy of Jesus Christ, the son of David, the son of Abraham" (1:1).

The genealogy that follows unfolds Israel's history beginning with Abraham and moving to David, then to exile, and then to the present day with Joseph, Mary, and Jesus. The opening sentence, though, signals that the author is concerned not only with historical succession but also with theological continuity. Both "son of David" and "son of Abraham" refer to central covenants that shape God's relationship with his people.

In this way, Matthew seems to deliberately position his following narrative about Jesus as a continuation of the history of redemption that began many years before.

2. *The Canonical Shape of the Sacred Scriptures:* This opening sequence also has structural similarities to key parts of the OT canon. This genealogy in the beginning of Matthew functions as a structural echo of the opening of Chronicles (1 Chron 1–9). The book of Chronicles is the only other biblical work in which a genealogy features so prominently at its beginning. This structural parallel to Chronicles introduces the notions

of exile, return from exile, and the hope of a coming "son of David" into the beginning of Matthew's narrative.

By using the phrase, "book of the genealogies," in Matt 1:1, Matthew alludes to the first book of the Hebrew Bible ("the book of the generations of Adam," Gen 5:1). By including a wide-ranging genealogy that emphasizes the role of David and the exile as an opening section (echoing the opening of Chronicles), Matthew also here alludes to one of the last books of the Hebrew Bible.

This genealogy in Matt 1, then, not only references Israel's historical past, but also communicates a network of textual and theological connections with the story of the Law, the Prophets, and the Writings.

With these connections, Matthew seems to imply that the proper context within which to read his message about Jesus is the Hebrew Bible as a whole. Taking seriously the possibility that Matt 1:1 ("book of the genealogies") and 1:2–17 (genealogy and exile) refer not only to historical realities but also textual entities, we can say that Matthew gives his readers a canon-conscious summary of the entire Hebrew Bible.

If asked how much of the OT is necessary to understand the story of Jesus most fully, Matthew here responds, "All of it!" Matthew urges his readers not only to remember biblical history, but also to read biblical texts.

3. *The Theological Rhythm of Promise & Fulfillment:* Broadening to the larger opening section of Matt 1–4, Matthew strikingly stops the narrative action at strategic locations to make a series of editorial comments. In these instances, he provides

a direct quotation with an introductory formula that emphasizes the fulfillment of Scriptural promises (1:22; 2:5–6; 2:15; 2:17–18; 2:23; 4:14–16).

Here specific events during the incarnation fulfill specific predictive promises and also "fill out" prophetic portraits of the coming Messiah's ministry.

These repeated statements that are clustered at the beginning of Matthew's narrative shed light on a profoundly theological aspect of biblical history. It's not only a chronological sequence but also a story of redemption being shaped by the Lord of history.

4. *A Rich Web of Intertextual Connections:* One final textual aspect to note in these opening chapters is the frequent and sophisticated literary links to Scriptural texts. Some of these are direct quotations that are explicitly noted by the author (like the quotation pattern noted above). Some of them are indirect allusions, where sentences or prominent phrases from an OT text are woven into the text of the Gospel.

For instance, when the voice of the Father speaks from heaven at Jesus's baptism, his divine statement is a blend of the wording from Ps 2 and Isa 42 (Matt 3:17 → Ps 2:7 & Isa 42:1). There are also more subtle echoes of OT texts, themes, and poetic images.

These connections are not usually marked directly but are communicated in more subtle and literary ways. For instance, if you're a close reader of the book of Moses, Matthew's portrayal of Jesus's temptation in the wilderness will likely give you a sense of literary *déjà vu* as you notice various points of contact with OT texts about the wilderness generation (e.g., the setting of the wilderness, the duration of forty years & forty days, texts quoted from a section of Deuteronomy that is itself providing a theological interpretation of the wilderness generation!, etc).

Each quotation, allusion, and echo is like another thread that binds together and forms the fabric of the broader biblical collection.

Relating the Testaments by Overhearing Hebrews

After briefly examining the opening chapters of Matthew's narrative, we can notice some of these same moves in a different kind of text like the letter to the Hebrews. This particular biblical text brims with rhetorical sophistication and has an extended theological argument. One of the author's chief compositional strategies is also near-constant reference to the OT Scriptures. Taking a 10k foot fly-over of this remarkable text can help us discern the contours of its biblical-theological moves.

In these Last Days:
The Grand Storyline of Redemptive History

In the majestic opening of the letter, the writer establishes the theological framework that the rest of the argument will draw upon. As the writer asserts,

Long ago, at many times and in many ways, God spoke to our fathers by the prophets, but in these last days he has spoken to us by his Son, whom he appointed the heir of all things, through whom also he created the world. He is the radiance of the glory of God and the exact imprint of his nature, and he upholds the universe by the word of his power. After making purification for sins, he sat down at the right hand of the Majesty on high, having become as much superior to angels as the name he has inherited is more excellent than theirs. (Heb 1:1–4)

In these few words, the writer masterfully pulls together many of the threads that the discipline of biblical theology seeks to explicate: the textual and theological relationship between the testaments; the nature of redemptive history; the grand storyline of the Bible; the person and work of Christ as the fulfillment of Scripture and the story of the covenants; and the relationship between the past, present, and future words and actions of God.

The same God who spoke "long ago" speaks "in these last days." The time of "our fathers" is connected to "us." The revelation "by the prophets" is connected to the revelation "by his Son." Of course, the letter to the Hebrews itself addresses these themes in a powerful and unique way throughout the rest of its "word of exhortation."

This intricate opening sentence previews what will unfold in the rest of the letter: a distinctive blend of complementary ways of relating different eras and varying aspects of redemptive history (seen especially in the multifaceted use of the OT).

There are several prominent places where the writer draws directly upon the grand storyline of redemptive history (which follows the contours of the OT's prophetic history). In these examples, the writer makes a point that requires the reader to think about the sequence and significance of some aspect of redemptive history.

For example, the frequent comparisons and contrasts between elements of the old covenant and the new covenant draw upon this theologically charged historical framework (e.g., Heb 2:1–4; 3:1–6). The incarnation is the centerpiece of this strategy. Jesus was made "for a little while" lower than the angels so that he could defeat death and bring "many sons to glory" after returning to his exalted position at the right hand of majesty (Heb 1:4; 2:8–10). Israel's wandering in the wilderness is the backdrop for the writer's warnings against unbelief, and the hope of peace in the land of promise is the primary analogy for the writer to exhort his readers to believe and enter God's rest (Heb 3–4).

In addition to the pervasive references to the exodus sequence, the writer also goes further back (to creation) and further forward (to entry into the land & the Davidic kingdom). These OT touchpoints provide a historical and theological framework for the writer to engage his audience in his own day and also envision the future reality of the eternal kingdom in God's presence (e.g., Heb 12:18–29!).[5]

In these Sacred Texts:
Overhearing a Host of Intertextual Voices

The grand storyline of the OT's portrayal of Israel's history provides the set pieces and literary landscape for the letter's drama. The quotations, allusions, and echoes of OT texts provide the soundtrack that brings to life the author's overarching argument. Hebrews is not a silent movie. It is a skillfully composed comprehensive musical filled with ancient melodies and familiar cadences alongside new notes and freshly revealed refrains.

To give only a few instances of the intertextual electricity that lights up this letter, consider the way that the dense opening sentence gives way to a flowing string of OT quotations. Seven major statements about *who the Son is* and *what the Son has done* (Heb 1:1–4) are followed by seven quotations of OT Scripture that are loaded with theological freight (Heb 1:5–14).

- The Son who is the radiance of the Father's glory is also the anointed son of Ps 2 and the promised descendent of 2 Sam 7.

- The Son who upholds the universe by his powerful word is also the psalmist's Lord and God.

- The one who has made purification for sins is also the one worthy of everyone's worship.

Rhetorically, this string of OT quotations in 1:5–14 gives the reader a chance to reflect on the significance of the compact statements about the person and work of the Son in 1:1–4.

In Heb 1:1–4, the writer alludes to Ps 2 (heir of all things) and then Ps 110 (seated at the right hand). In 1:5–14, the first quotation is from Ps 2 ("You are my Son") and then the final quotation is from Ps 110 ("Sit at my right hand").

Confirming the structural significance of these texts for the message of the letter as a whole, the opening of the second major movement in Heb 5 contains another quotation of these texts in this same sequence (Ps 2 in 5:5, and this time Ps 110:4 in 5:6).

In large measure, the letter as a whole hinges on these textual connections: The writer gives a theological interpretation of

Ps 2 & Ps 110 as a lens through which to grasp the full significance of the mission of the Son in the incarnation.

In Heb 2, the author quotes Ps 8 at length and then reflects at length on its significance. In Heb 3, the writer quotes Ps 95 in order to emphasize the promise of God's wrath, and in Heb 4, the writer quotes the same psalm in order to emphasize the promise of God's rest.

In Heb 8, the author gives a long quotation of Jeremiah in order to make a point about the nature of the new covenant. By contrast to Heb 2, there is only a minimal follow-up exposition, as the quoted text makes the point the writer wants to emphasize directly. In Heb 11, the writer weaves together summaries of Israel's history with strategic quotations of Israel's texts.

Hearing and Seeing More Than Once

Much more could be said about the function of redemptive history and the use of the OT in Hebrews (mountains of scholarship in fact!), but one thing we've seen clearly is that the writer provides several distinctive angles on the relationship between the old and the new (OT & NT, old covenant & new covenant, eternity past & eternity future, etc!).

As readers of this remarkable and engaging text, we are invited to gaze along these sight lines as we behold the glory of God in Christ by his Spirit.

It seems like the biblical authors equip and expect us to hear these words and see these sights in multiple ways and more than once.

The Biblical Canon as a Majestic Mountain Range

There are many interpretive issues to examine for each of these connections I've noted here, but for our purpose we can note that both Matthew and Hebrews give us several different kinds of tools for relating the testimony of the OT and the gospel proclamation of the NT. Each of the categories above has also been proposed as normative ways of characterizing the relationship between the testaments.

The point we're making here is that the texts of the NT seem to employ several complementary ways of construing this relationship. While these categories are sometimes played off of one another, it's more fruitful to see them as distinct angles that open up unique lines of sight for biblical readers to behold.

The literary landscape of the biblical canon is like a majestic mountain range. Each of these biblical-theological trajectories is like a map to a specific pathway through this scenic countryside that you are invited to traverse as a dedicated reader. Sure, you can pick one of these paths and only hike along its tracks. This will allow you to get to know the area really well, and you'll come to know those trails like the back of your hand. But part of the wonder of a mountain range is that it requires a variety of vantage points to be known in its fullness.

Imagine walking for hours on a tree-laden trail to make it to the summit that opens onto a wide-ranging panoramic view. The trail helps you see the granular features of the terrain. You also get to experience it yourself as you trod along its path with your own two feet. The panoramic overview does not add any dimensions to the mountain you've just traversed, but it does give you a perspective that would be impossible without its vantage point.

In our study so far, we've looked at just a few of the main textual trails one might take across the highways and byways of the biblical canon. There is a grand storyline that includes the story of the prophets and the proclamation of the apostles. Biblical books have been shaped as meaningful texts that have been collected in a canonical context. There is a rhythm of promise and fulfillment across the unfolding of redemptive history. There is a rich web of textual connections that hold together the vibrant and complex tapestry of the Bible's "big picture."

Just like you will never fully exhaust the dimensions of a majestic mountain range, these kinds of paths across the literary landscape of the biblical canon provide a blueprint for a lifetime of life-giving exploration and reflection.

Discussion & Reflection

1. What has been your experience with the OT? Have you always had a sense that it was important, or do you struggle to see its relevance? Do you typically stay anchored in the NT for your reading and devotion?

2. Why do you think the OT is so important for Jesus and the NT authors? This emphasis would have been especially relevant to the Jewish community that first heard this message, but the NT authors also spoke of the OT just as much when they preached the gospel in Gentile contexts. How could a study of the OT help you understand the NT and the gospel message?

3. Read and reflect on Matt 1 and Heb 11. Both of these passages draw on the biblical storyline, allude to OT texts, and also make connections to new covenant teaching. Compare and contrast the way that Matthew and the writer of Hebrews make use of the OT. How is the OT a springboard for their message about Jesus?

Notes:

1. For a fuller discussion of the phrase "two testaments to tell" and the main argument of this chapter, see Spellman, "Two Testaments to Tell: Biblical Theology and the Canonical Shape of the Gospel," *Journal of Theological Interpretation* (2024); and Spellman, *Invitation to BT*, 82–89.

2. The term "kergyma" (*kerr igh mah*) comes from the Greek word that is translated "to preach" or "to proclaim." In biblical studies, kerygma refers to the "preached word" of the Apostles as seen in the NT. Though it's a technical term, it's worth knowing (because it helpfully connects the content of the gospel message with the act of proclaiming it).

3. In Acts 2:16–21, Peter cites Joel 2:28–32. In 2:31, he cites Ps 16:10. In 2:34, he cites Ps 110:1.

4. The texts Paul cites are Ps 2:7, Isa 55:3, Ps 16:10, and Hab 1:5. On the next Sabbath (Acts 13:44–49), Paul and Barnabas explain the Gentile mission with reference to Isa 49:6.

5. Much more could be said about the way Hebrews draws upon the flow of redemptive history as the author makes textual connections and theological arguments. Particularly relevant in this regard are the treatments of Joshua & David in Heb 4:1–10, Abraham & Melchizedek in Heb 7:1–10, and the "hall of faith" in Heb 11.

6

The Great Hero of this Grand Storyline
Remembering the Risen Son of David

The Christology of the Christian canon is like a shimmering diamond with multiple facets and numerous cutting edges.

Biblical theology aims to allow us to discern the contours of these edges so that we are able to see the richness of God's revelation as it refracts through the light of his glory.

In our study so far, we have examined many of the biblical-theological features of the grand storyline of the Bible and the far-reaching implications of the compositional strategies of the biblical authors. This hard work is part of what allows us to behold the canonical portrait of Christ with joyful clarity.

One angle of sight that is particularly helpful is the fourth Gospel's richly intertextual theology of the person and work of Jesus. With a profound attention to the meaning of OT texts and the comprehensive sweep of redemptive history, the Gospel of John draws upon and deepens the theological interpretation that we find in Matthew, Mark, and Luke. This narrative culminates the fourfold Gospel and draws together many biblical-theological threads.

The Great Hero of John's Gospel:
A Lion of Judah and a Lamb who was Slain

The Gospel starts by quickly establishing the divine person and redemptive work of Jesus. As John writes, "In the beginning was the Word, and the Word was with God, and the Word was God. He was in the beginning with God" (Jn 1:1–2). John here alludes to the creation narrative of Gen 1. By doing so, John connects the story of the Gospel to the story of the OT in the most majestic way possible.

This story John tells (or rather continues) begins before the foundation of the world. John's biblical-theological prologue prepares for his thickly theological account of the incarnation: "And the Word became flesh and dwelt among us, and we have seen his glory, glory as of the only Son from the Father, full of grace and truth" (Jn 1:14). As with the other Gospels, following his orienting reflection John refers to "the Word who became flesh" simply as "Jesus" for the rest of his Gospel. The reader must decide what they will make of this Jesus.

John articulates his literary purpose along these same lines at the end of his narrative. He writes, "Now Jesus did many other signs in the presence of the disciples, which are not written in this book; but these are written so that you may believe that Jesus is the Christ, the Son of God, and that by believing you may have life in his name" (Jn 20:30–31). Similar to Matthew's purpose expressed in Matt 1:1, John here mentions writing a "book" designed to convince readers that Jesus is "the Christ, the Son of God."

Although he never uses the Davidic title in the same way Matthew, Mark, and Luke do, John draws on significant

Davidic texts and images in his portrayal of Jesus as the messianic King of Israel. In fact, the center of John's presentation of the death of Jesus as the fulfillment of the Scriptures lies in identifying him as the true and better David. Accordingly, one critical component of John's strategy in his Gospel entails demonstrating that Jesus is the Davidic shepherd-king of Israel whose suffering and death fulfills the Scriptures.

Jesus as the Davidic King

At the beginning of his crucifixion narrative, John portrays Jesus as the Davidic King. After Jesus carries his cross to Golgotha, he is crucified between two other men (19:17–18). There, Pilate writes an inscription and places it upon the cross that reads, "Jesus of Nazareth, the King of the Jews" (19:19). John notes that many Jews read the inscription because the cross was near the city and the sign was written in three languages (Hebrew, Greek, and Latin).

Because the title was so prominent, the chief priests ask Pilate not to write "King of the Jews" since Jesus had only claimed that, "I am the King of the Jews" (19:21). By drawing out this discourse, John allows for emphatic repetition of the title, "King of the Jews." Pilate responds to this inquiry by invoking his perceived final authority: "What I have written I have written" (19:22).

Before the crucifixion, John highlights the conversation that takes place between Jesus and Pilate regarding Jesus's status as king. After the Jews bring their prisoner to him, Pilate questions Jesus's kingship by asking, "Are you the King of the Jews?" (18:33). From this point until the actual crucifixion,

John carefully traces the way Pilate consistently raises this issue with the Jews and Jesus himself. In these exchanges, the nature of Jesus's kingdom is outlined. After questioning Pilate's motivation for asking about his kingship (18:34), Jesus reveals that his kingdom is otherworldly. If his kingdom was of this world, his servants would be fighting so that Jesus would not be handed over to the Jews. As it is, his kingdom is "not from the world" (18:36).

Pilate recognizes the significance of Jesus's claims and asks, "So you are a king?" Jesus responds, "You say correctly that I am a king" (18:37, NASB). Alluding to his messianic mission, Jesus conveys that "for this purpose I was born and for this purpose I have come into the world—to bear witness to the truth" (18:37). After hearing this, Pilate again offers the Jews a chance to release their "king" (18:39). Rather than release their "lawful" king, the Jews choose to free the robber Barabbas. In a scene fraught with irony, the soldiers then scourge and mock their Jewish prisoner. Because of Jesus's alleged royalty, the soldiers twist together a crown of thorns and give him a purple robe, sarcastically hailing him as "King of the Jews!" (19:3).

These words highlight the irony of the scene, as the soldiers pronounce in derision what should be on the lips of the Jews in devotion. Rather than bowing before him, they bring him blows.

After the Jews insist that Pilate execute this man, Pilate engages Jesus in further dialogue. Though Pilate positions himself as the superior ruler, Jesus undermines Pilate's authority and asserts his own. When Jesus does not answer the governor's question regarding where he is from, Pilate stresses his power: "Do you not know that I have authority to release you and authority to crucify you?" (19:10). Jesus reverses his logic by asserting that Pilate "would have no authority" over him unless it had been given from above (19:11). Pilate responds by trying again to release him, but the Jews argue that releasing an imposter king would make Pilate no friend of Caesar (19:12).

Despite the politically expedient argument of the Jews, John's narrative still focuses on the debate over Jesus's kingship. Sitting down on his "judgment seat," Pilate exclaims "Behold, your King!" and asks once more, "Shall I crucify your King?" The chief priests then solidify their theological treason by answering, "We have no king but Caesar" (19:14–15). Thus, the man identified as the King of the Jews by a pagan Gentile ruler is crucified by his own people. In his account of Jesus before Pilate, John illustrates the way the true king of Israel "came to his own, and his own people did not receive him" (1:10).

There are two other important places in the Gospel where John applies the expectation of a coming king to Jesus. In the account of Jesus calling his disciples (1:43–51), John highlights the messianic expectation of a coming one foretold in the "Law and also the prophets" (1:45). After Jesus tells Nathaniel that he saw him under the fig tree, Nathaniel exclaims, "Rabbi, you are the Son of God! You are the King of Israel!" (1:49). This reference to the King of Israel clearly demonstrates that a significant aspect of messianic expectation included the anticipation of a coming king.

John revisits this expectation in his account of Jesus's entry into Jerusalem (John 12). After Mary anoints him in Bethany, Jesus enters Jerusalem. Hearing of his arrival, a large crowd comes out to meet him armed with palm branches and the words of Ps 118. They cry out, "Hosanna! Blessed is he who comes in the name of the Lord, even the King of Israel!" (12:13). This declaration of the people connects the words of Ps 118:26 with expectations concerning the coming King of Israel. In John's account, the "one who comes in the name of the Lord" is the coming king.

John immediately follows these words with the detail that Jesus rides upon a young donkey into the city (alluding to the messianic portrayal in Zech 9:9–10). John's account here is brief but significant, for it keeps the kingship of Jesus in front of the reader.

Jesus as the Davidic Shepherd

After Jesus is crucified and pierced by the soldier's spear, John notes how this fulfills the Scripture that says, "They will look on him whom they have pierced" (Jn 19:37). John's reference to Zech 12:10 here resonates not only with his earlier emphasis on the Davidic kingship in John 18, but also with his use of Davidic shepherd imagery.

The "pierced one" of Zechariah's prophetic vision is associated with both a king and a shepherd. In Zech 9, Zechariah describes the Lord saving Israel as "the flock of His people" (9:16). Because of false dreams and vain comfort, the people will "wander like sheep" who are afflicted "because there is no shepherd" (Zech 10:2). Those shepherding Israel have angered the Lord of Hosts because they have neglected "his flock, the house of Judah" (10:3). As the good shepherd, the Lord will "whistle" and gather his redeemed sheep, the ones he scattered in order to gather to himself again (10:8–12).

Using this shepherd imagery, the Lord directs Zechariah to "pasture the flock doomed to slaughter" (11:4). Zechariah thus represents the Lord as the shepherd of the people, but his guidance is rejected. In a reversal of the imagery of the good shepherd, the Lord then directs Zechariah to embody the "foolish shepherd" who will "not care for the perishing, seek the scattered, heal the broken, or sustain the one standing" (11:15–16). This "worthless shepherd" not only leaves the sheep, but is also incapable of guiding and protecting the flock (11:17).

In this context, the Lord describes to Zechariah a day when Jerusalem will be attacked (Zech 12:1–5) but will ultimately be delivered by the Lord (12:6–9). On that day, the Lord will set about to "destroy all the nations that come against Jerusalem" (12:9). In the midst of this restoration, the house of David and the people of Jerusalem will mourn their sin and idolatry (12:11–14). Those who speak false prophecies will also grieve and be ashamed of their deceptive visions (13:1–6). Though the people will recognize their depravity, the Lord will nevertheless pour out on them "a Spirit of grace and pleas for mercy" that will enable them to look "on me, on him whom they have pierced" (12:10).

They will mourn and bitterly weep over this pierced one "as one mourns for an only child" (12:10). This pierced one resembles the shepherd struck down in Zech 13:7. There the Lord declares, "Awake, O sword, against my Shepherd" and orders, "Strike the Shepherd that the sheep may be scattered" (13:7). These words echo the words of Zech 10:9–10 and show how they will be accomplished. The Lord will scatter the sheep by striking the shepherd.

This event will cause them to call on his name, and he will answer them (13:9). Thus, though the shepherd is struck down and the sheep scatter, the Lord will enable the people to "look on him" with mourning and repentance, resulting in their eventual and ultimate redemption.[1]

In a broad sense, the shepherd imagery utilized in Zech 9–13 resonates with John's narrative. In Jn 10:1–30, John gives sustained attention to Jesus's teaching that he is the good shepherd. In the first part of the chapter, Jesus outlines how a shepherd protects his sheep from strangers, thieves, and robbers. In this "figure of speech" (Jn 10:6), the contrast between the shepherd and other people is striking. The sheep follow only the voice of the shepherd, and only the shepherd knows them and guides them to safety (10:3–4).

After painting this pastoral scene, Jesus makes direct use of this imagery. He asserts that he is "the door of the sheep" (10:7) in that those who enter through him will be saved (10:9). The sheep will find rest and shelter in him as they go in and out to find pasture. Carrying the metaphor further, Jesus states he is not only the door of the sheep, but also the guardian of that door. Bringing this metaphor to a climax, Jesus declares, "I am the good shepherd" (10:11).

He then expounds his role as that figure. The good shepherd lays down his life "for the sheep" (10:11). Rather than fleeing at the sight of danger like a hired hand (10:12–13), the "good shepherd" is concerned about his sheep and says, "I know my own and my own know me" (10:14). This good shepherd knows and is known by the Father (10:15). Because the shepherd lays down his life and takes it up again for the sake of the sheep, the Father loves him (10:17). The shepherd also has the task of bringing in the "other sheep" who are "not of this fold." The goal of the shepherd's mission is to form "one flock" that has "one shepherd" (10:16).

John confirms the messianic nature of this shepherd imagery in 10:22–30. After Jesus's words incur a division among the Jews (10:19–21), they gather around Jesus and ask, "How long will you keep us in suspense? If you are the Christ, tell us plainly" (10:24). Jesus responds, "I told you, and you did not believe" (10:25). To explain this unbelief, Jesus again casts himself as the shepherd. The Jews did not believe because they were not of his sheep. The sheep hear his voice, he knows them, and they follow him (10:27). The sheep are given to him by the Father and are eternally secure in the shepherd's hand (10:28–30).

Thus, Jesus responds to the question concerning the identity of the Christ by essentially reasserting that he is the good shepherd. Jesus implies that when he told the Jews that he was the good shepherd, he was in fact telling them he was the Christ. The reason why Jesus's logic makes sense is because shepherd imagery is part of the messianic tapestry developed in the prophets of the Hebrew Bible.[2]

Thus, when Jesus speaks of himself as the good shepherd, he draws upon a strong messianic image from the OT. A close reader of the Hebrew Bible will also note that John's quotation of Zech 12:10 in John 19 combines these messianic pastoral images with the messianic kingship images of the trial in John 18. The piercing passage is particularly appropriate for John at this point in his narrative, since both the shepherd and king images are prominent in that portion of Zechariah. As we have seen above, the same images are also prominent throughout John's narrative.[3]

The immediate connection John makes in Jn 19:37 regards the specific detail of Jesus's pierced side. Though there is some ambiguity in Zech 12:10 regarding the identity of the figure who is pierced,[4] there is no ambiguity for John: the pierced one whom Israel looks upon is Jesus, the Christ. By quoting these words, John identifies Jesus as the promised one of messianic prophecy. By connecting the piercing of Jesus to the "pierced one" of Zechariah's prophecy, John ends his crucifixion narrative by demonstrating that Jesus is the Davidic shepherd-king who is being struck down in order to gather his scattered people.

The Death of the Davidic Shepherd-King Fulfills the Scriptures

In the midst of these two vibrant Davidic images that coalesce in the crucifixion narrative, John demonstrates that the details of Jesus's crucifixion fulfill specific Davidic psalms. The first detail concerns what happens to Jesus's clothes (19:23–25).

After the soldiers crucify Jesus, they divide his outer garments amongst themselves. John notes that Jesus's tunic was seamless, "woven in one piece" (19:23). Instead of tearing it, they "cast lots for it" (19:24). John records that the soldiers "did these things" in order "to fulfill the Scripture." He then quotes Ps 22:18: "They divided my outer garments among them, and for my clothing they cast lots."

In a striking way, John asserts that this specific element of Jesus's crucifixion corresponds to the scene depicted in Ps 22. Several other specific details in Ps 22 correspond to John's crucifixion account and further highlight his interest in demonstrating this intertextual connection. These include Jesus's thirst (Jn 19:28/Ps 22:15), his pierced hands and feet (Jn 19:23/Ps 22:16), and his preserved bones (Jn 19:33/Ps 22:17).

Further resonance can be found between Ps 69 and Jesus's thirst on the cross. After Jesus entrusts his mother Mary to "the disciple whom he loved" (19:25b–27), he exclaims, "I am thirsty." John records that Jesus knew that "all things had already been accomplished" and spoke these words in order "to fulfill the Scripture" (19:28). Jesus's indication of his thirst matches the details of the scene presented in Ps 69. There the psalmist writes, "They gave me poison for food, and for my thirst they gave me sour wine to drink" (Ps 69:21). Accordingly, John recounts that "a jar full of sour wine stood there" (19:29). The soldiers take a sponge full of this sour wine and lift it to Jesus's mouth using a branch of hyssop. After receiving the sour wine, Jesus says, "It is finished!" and, bowing his head, gives up his spirit (19:30).

By recording Jesus's statement, "I am thirsty," John makes a thematic allusion to Ps 69. By referencing this text alongside Ps 22, John asserts that what Jesus "finished" on the cross was completely in line with "the Scriptures." Indeed, this accomplished work fulfills the Scriptures and fills out the messianic vision of these psalms down to the seemingly trivial details concerning the disposal of garments and distribution of sour wine.

The final detail relates to Jesus's bones remaining unbroken (19:31–36). John recounts that the Jews wanted the bodies taken down from the crosses because it was the day of preparation and the Sabbath was drawing near (19:31). However, when the soldiers came to break Jesus's legs, "they saw that he was already dead" and did not break any of his bones (19:32–33). Perhaps to guarantee Jesus was truly dead, one of the soldiers "pierced his side with a spear," which immediately caused blood and water to flow from his body (19:34). John asserts one last time that these things came to pass to fulfill Scripture.

In addition to the piercing of Jesus's side fulfilling Zech 12:10, John asserts that the preservation of Jesus's bones fulfilled the Scripture that "not one of his bones will be broken" (19:36). This statement has strong Passover connotations (Exod 12:46; Num 9:12), and also relates to John's conviction that Jesus fulfills and replaces the role of the Passover lamb.

Additionally, these words resonate with Ps 34:20. In Ps 34, David reflects on the Lord's deliverance of the righteous by saying, "He keeps all his bones, not one of them is broken" (34:20). This reflection made by David in the midst of his suffering is filled out in the details of what happens to Jesus on the cross.

In this way, John demonstrates that even the details of Jesus's passion go according to plan. By referencing the Psalms, John interprets a scene of seemingly meaningless brutality. Rather than merely an execution planned by indignant religious leaders and carried out by a complicit Roman government, John demonstrates that the death of Israel's Messiah falls within the design of divine providence. Even its smallest details have been prefigured in the words of the Davidic Psalms.

John's scene does not depict abandonment, but rather fulfillment. Additionally, the Passover connections point to the saving nature of Jesus's sacrificial death, while the

Davidic connections stress that the Lord has not abandoned his Messiah, even as he is murdered.

Concluding Reflections

By highlighting the king and shepherd motifs, John employs two of the most significant Davidic images available to him from the Hebrew Scriptures. John writes his Gospel so that the reader might believe that Jesus is the Christ (Jn 20:30–31). In other words, the Son of God is also the Son of David.

This emphasis also has an implication for the fourfold Gospel collection. John's portrayal of Jesus as the Davidic messiah connects with Matthew's clear emphasis on Jesus as the "Son of David" (Matt 1:1). Matthew focuses on the Davidic title "Son of David" and primarily uses allusions in his references to the Psalms in his crucifixion account (Matt 27).

Conversely, John chooses to focus on Davidic images in his narrative rather than the Davidic title, but makes direct quotations of the Davidic Psalms in his passion account (John 19). John also uses explicit fulfillment language in reference to the manner in which David's life anticipates and prefigures the life of Jesus the Messiah.

Rather than pitting these two compositional strategies against each other, one might view them in a more interconnected way. Matthew raises the "Son of David" question in a striking manner and consistently keeps before the reader the question, "Could this be the Son of David?" (Matt 12:23). Matthew raises the David issue by directing focus upon the title, and John picks up on this motif and fills out the rest of the picture by ending his Gospel with a flurry of kingly discourse.

Whereas Matthew addresses the question, "Could this be the Son of David?" John asks, "Is this the King of Israel?" Both authors answer in the affirmative and demonstrate that this Son of David is in fact the King of Israel.

The emphasis on and development of Jesus as the Davidic Messiah is thus one of the textual and thematic elements that draw the Gospels as a whole together.

As readers of the grand storyline of the Bible, we are not left without a witness to the purpose and identity of our rescuer. The Gospels enable us to know and trust "our great God and Savior Jesus Christ" (Titus 2:13).

Discussion & Reflection:

1. What comfort can we gain by reflecting on the fact that Jesus describes himself as the good shepherd? Read Ezek 37:24–28. Along with the Zechariah passages described above, how might these OT texts deepen this comfort?

2. Why is it important that Jesus is not only the good shepherd but also the shepherd-*king*?

3. John uses the Psalms to show us that Jesus fulfills the Scriptures. Throughout his ministry and at the most painful moments of his earthly life, Jesus also speaks these words himself. What psalms have helped you in your study of Scripture or in your own personal life?

Notes:

1. Ultimate redemption is implied in 13:9: "I will say, 'They are my people,' And they will say, 'The Lord is my God.'" This is the language of covenant promises.
2. In addition to the aforementioned texts in Zechariah, the book of Ezekiel contains some of the most developed shepherd imagery connected to messianic expectation. In Ezek 34 and 37, the coming Messiah is cast as a Davidic shepherd-king who will restore the hopes of Israel. In this eschatological vision, Israel will live in the land, David will rule over them forever, and the Lord will dwell in their midst forever, having made an everlasting covenant of peace with them (34:25–28). The coming rule of this Davidic shepherd-king will be the fulfillment and culmination of the promises made in the biblical covenants.
3. Piercing imagery (Zech 12:10/Jn 19:37) and striking imagery (Zech 13:7/Jn 19:3) are also present in both contexts.
4. Identifying the "pierced one" of Zech 12:10 is a notoriously difficult interpretive issue. For our purposes, it is enough to note that the pierced one is closely associated with the messianic images of its surrounding context (i.e., king and shepherd).

7

The Goal of this Grand Storyline
The Beginning and End of All Things

> "I'm glad that you are here with me. Here at the end of all things" (Sam to Frodo, *Return of the King*).

The beginning and end of the grand storyline of the Bible hold the keys that unlock its powerful message. The opening chapters of Genesis and the closing chapters of Revelation play a special role in the mental architecture of our view of God's cosmic plan for the world.

As the symphony of Scripture reaches a crescendo, we finally hear the layered harmony of resonating melody lines and the rhythm of familiar refrains. The beginning strikes a chord that finally resolves in this vision of the end.

In chapter 5, we looked at how the gospel is a story that takes two testaments to tell. In chapter 6, we saw the way that John's Gospel draws upon this canonical context to speak of Christ as the Davidic shepherd-king who lays his life down for his sheep. In this chapter, we continue this biblical-theological reflection by exploring how the Bible speaks of the purpose or goal of redemptive history.

The book of Revelation has a special place in the biblical canon and serves as a structuring element for the grand storyline of the Bible. Paying careful attention to its message as a coherent work allows us to see connections to a host of biblical texts, central themes, and narrative patterns that help us make sense of what we read in God's word and experience in God's world.

Revelation as a Fitting Conclusion to the Grand Storyline

One of the important points to make about the book of Revelation is its basic narrative framework. Here at the end of the NT collection, we receive a final revelation from the resurrected Christ. The book has a narrative framework that includes a commission from Jesus to one of his apostles, letters to seven churches, allusions to the beginning of all things, and a vision of the end of all things.

Revelation is situated at the close of the NT canon to provide a remarkably cohesive account of the past, present, and future work of God in the world and how believers should function in light of this all-encompassing vision of reality.

One of the clear ways that this book helps us see the coherence of the grand storyline of the Bible as a whole is the way that it ends. The last chapters of Revelation will likely remind you of the first chapters of the book of Genesis. Indeed, the narratives of Gen 1–3 are of critical importance for the biblical storyline and the resulting biblical meta-narrative (i.e., worldview). Important themes mentioned here are developed throughout the OT and NT.

Genesis begins with the creation of the heavens and the earth (Gen 1:1), and Revelation ends with the creation of a new heaven and a new earth (Rev 21:1). In the final chapters of his book, John explores how the work of God in the risen Christ brings about the renewal of all creation, the restoration of God's original purpose for humanity, and the enduring promise of a coming redeemer.

Each of these themes is supported by verbal, thematic, or structural links to significant texts from the Hebrew Bible. In particular, through a network of intertextual allusions to the narratives of Gen 1–3, John creates in Rev 21–22 a book-length bookend for the biblical canon and its multifaceted storyline.

Renewed Creation

After the judgment at the great white throne (Rev 20:11–15), John recounts, "Then I saw a new heaven and a new earth" (21:1). Next, John sees "the holy city, new Jerusalem, coming down out of heaven from God, prepared as a bride adorned for her husband" (21:2). After this creative event, "a loud voice from the throne" provides an interpretation of what John has just seen which emphasizes the incredible effect the divine presence has on the worship of God's people (21:3–4).

In the following paragraph, this "loud voice from the throne" makes a summary pronouncement over this new creation: "Behold, I am making all things new." John is again commanded to "write this down, for these words are trustworthy and true" (21:5). God then tells John with a note of finality, "It is done. I am the Alpha and the Omega, the beginning and the end." Thus ends the sequence of creative actions in these last chapters of Revelation.

The remainder of Rev 21 describes and explains the new creation that takes place in 21:1–5. After proclaiming the completion of the new creation, God offers blessings for those who believe and overcome but curses for those who are cowardly and do not believe (21:7). After beholding God fashion the new creation, John gets a guided tour of the new Jerusalem (21:10–27), including the river of the water of life and the tree of life (22:1–2). The pastoral imagery and heavenly vision of Rev 21:1–22:5 is set within the framework of God's creative activity.

This theme of creation is foundational for much of the biblical and prophetic understanding of the world. God as creator of the heavens and the earth is one of the most important characterizations of Israel's God. Accordingly, the idea of a new creation is just as important and builds upon the theology of God as creator.

Just as in the Genesis account, "he who was seated on the throne" in Rev 21:5 speaks and all things are made new: "Behold, I am making all things new."

Renewed Worship

Continuing the parallel with the creation narratives, Rev 21 displays a scene that essentially fills out the original purpose of creation. Before the fall into sin described in Gen 3, a snapshot of the purpose of mankind on the earth is provided in Gen 2. Adam and Eve are placed in the garden to serve God, enjoy his presence, and worship and obey their creator.

The scene in Gen 2 indicates humanity's created purpose. After creating Adam, the Lord God places the man in the Garden of Eden in order "to work it and keep it" (Gen 2:15). The verbs in this phrase that are usually translated as "work" and "keep" are elsewhere used to describe the worship of

Israel, specifically the priestly "service" and "guarding" of the tabernacle.[1]

By using these terms, the author of Genesis shows that one of humanity's created purposes is to worship and obey the Lord by keeping his commands and guarding his covenant relationship with them. They were to be God's people, and the Lord was to be their God.

This purpose is the foundational element of the various covenant relationships that occur in subsequent biblical narratives. The Garden of Eden was intended to be the place where God met with his people. The later OT institutions of the tabernacle and the temple were intended to serve a similar worship-oriented function. The garden, the tabernacle, and the temple are all means by which God could be present among his people.

In his account of the eschatological recreation in Rev 21–22, John makes use of all three of these sacred locations. After beholding the new heaven and earth (21:1), John sees "the holy city, new Jerusalem, coming down out of heaven from God" (21:2). The covenantal overtones are indicated by the use of marriage imagery. The holy city has been "prepared as a bride adorned for her husband" (21:2).[2]

The new Jerusalem represents God's divine presence. The portrayal of the new Jerusalem in Rev 21:10–21 draws on prophetic descriptions of the future temple.[3] The details of this description reveal that the city has been constructed with the most precious of materials. Everything in the new Jerusalem demonstrates its exceeding value and worth.

However, the rarity and worth of the city is ultimately derived from the one who dwells there: God himself. The brilliance of the city is rightly seen only in relation to its most profound characteristic, namely "the glory of God" (21:11).

That the portrayal and purpose of the holy city points to God's divine presence with his people is confirmed by references to the tabernacle and the temple after this description of the new Jerusalem. In Rev 21:3, John hears a voice say, "Behold, the tabernacle of God is among men" (NASB). This voice provides another expression of covenantal relationship by saying that "he will dwell with them, and they will be his people, and God himself will be with them as their God" (21:3).

After the description of the city (21:10–21), John notes the absence of a temple in its midst: "I saw no temple in the city." John explains that the divine presence removes the need for a temple. He reasons, "For its temple is the Lord God the Almighty and the Lamb" (21:22).

The new Jerusalem also no longer needs the light of the sun or the moon, "for the glory of God gives it light, and its lamp is the Lamb" (21:23). This detail regarding the obsolete function of the sun and the moon indicates that the new creation far surpasses the old creation. Whereas before the sun and moon lit up the world of humankind, the Lamb who was slain for them now performs that function.

This is a profound fulfillment of what John says in the prologue of his Gospel: "The true light, which gives light to everyone, was coming into the world" (Jn 1:9). This light illumines not only Israel, but also the nations who will walk "by its light" and the kings of the earth who will "bring their glory into it" (Rev 21:24). The illumination of the divine presence reorders the way the universe works.

Renewed Eden

Another striking element of this new creation is the removal of sin and the reversal of the curse. In Rev 22, John is shown the "river of the water of life, bright as crystal, flowing from the throne of God and of the Lamb through the middle of the street of the city" (22:1–2). Alongside this crystal-clear river is "the tree of life" that bears twelve kinds of fruit which it yields every month. This idyllic scene strongly echoes the picture of the Garden of Eden in Gen 2.

However, this new garden is altogether different, for here there is no serpent lurking in the shadows.[4] The leaves of this tree of life no longer recall transgression, but are "for the healing of the nations" (22:2).

Whereas Gen 3 recounts the consequences of disobedience among the trees in the garden, on this day "there will no longer be any curse" (Rev 22:3, NASB). The eschatological garden will be the throne room of God and the Lamb, and "his servants will worship him" (22:3).

This reversal of the effects of the curse is anticipated in Rev 21:4–5. Acknowledging the pain and suffering that has taken place between the Garden of Eden and the new Jerusalem, the voice tells John that God "will wipe away every tear from their eyes" and "death shall be no more, neither shall there be mourning, nor crying, nor pain anymore, for the former things have passed away" (21:4).

This scene paints a picture of the fulfillment of the new covenant. Sins have been forgiven, pain is no more, and the curse has been reversed. In short, paradise has been restored.

Renewed Promise

A final connection between Rev 21–22 and Gen 1–3 involves the identification of the one who accomplishes this redemption. Revelation makes clear that the work of the Lamb is the sole reason God's people are able to experience his presence in this new creation. In Rev 1, the Lamb is the one who has "has freed us from our sins by his blood" (Rev 1:5). John's vision reveals that this Lamb of God is also the Lion of Judah. John recounts in Rev 5:5 that Jesus is "the Lion that is from the tribe of Judah, the Root of David."

These references to "the Lion of Judah" and "the Root of David" are clear thematic allusions to messianic texts of the OT.[5] Later, in Rev 22:16, Jesus declares, "I am the root and the descendent of David, the bright morning star." This characterization of Jesus strongly resonates with the expectations found in the story of the Hebrew Bible concerning the coming Davidic king.

The anticipation of a coming king from the tribe of Judah who will crush God's enemies, rule in power, and receive the obedience of the people stems from promises of the Pentateuch (e.g., Gen 49:8–10; Num 24:7–9).

This kingly expectation is later joined with God's covenant promise to David in 2 Sam 7. The coming king of the Pentateuch will be a son of David. In the story of the Law, the Prophets, and the Writings, the eschatological King of Israel comes from David's seed.

Accordingly, in the Hebrew Bible, when the coming king is mentioned, the eschatological son of David is usually in view, or at least lurking nearby. Jesus's final words in Revelation point us to this theologically explosive network of connections.

Bringing it All Together in the End

By strategically identifying Jesus as the son of David, John adopts an important biblical image. One of the purposes of the vision of Revelation is to "fill out" this prophetic portrayal of Jesus as the reigning Davidic king. As the voices in the heavenly court proclaim in Rev 11:15, John's vision anticipates the moment when "the kingdom of the world has become the kingdom of our Lord and of his Christ, and he shall reign forever and ever."

Just as John's Gospel showed how Jesus's crucifixion filled out the scene of the suffering servant of Ps 22, here John's Apocalypse shows how Jesus's exaltation fills out the scene of the reigning son of Ps 2.

Just as the focus on Jesus as the Christ ties the book of Revelation to the rest of the NT, so too this emphasis binds it to the story of the OT. Indeed, the revelation of Jesus as the prophesied Davidic Messiah might be "the canonical integrating element within the whole of the OT and the NT."[6]

Only in this coming king is the hope of a new creation and a new life made a reality.

Discussion & Reflection

1. With some books or films, knowing the details of how it all ends makes any repeated reading or viewing less enjoyable (spoiler alert!). For other stories, you have to experience them multiple times to really get what's going on. In what ways are biblical books the kind of texts that deepen and expand the more you read and reflect upon them?

2. What are some of the central themes of BT that you see in both the beginning of Genesis and the end of Revelation?

3. What is your favorite textual detail in John's vision of the new creation in Rev 21–22? Why does this detail stand out to you?

Notes:

1. For example, see Num 3:7–8; 8:25–26; 18:5–6; 1 Chron 23:32; Ezek 44:14.

2. Note the connection between a marriage at the beginning of the Bible (Gen 2) and a marriage at the end of the Bible (Rev 19; 21). Isa 61:10 and 62:5 pick up the marriage imagery as well.

3. The details John records regarding the holy city are imbued with imagery from Ezek 40–48.

4. In Rev 12:9, John identifies "the great dragon" who was thrown down out of heaven as "the serpent of old who is called the devil and Satan, who deceives the whole world." This same "serpent of old" is bound for a thousand years in 20:2, and then in 20:10 is thrown into the lake of fire to be "tormented day and night forever and ever." Thus, readers of Revelation will know at this point in the book why there is no serpent found in this eschatological garden.

5. The "Lion of Judah" phrase is drawn from Gen 49:9, and the "Root of David" comes from Isa 11:1, 10 (cf. Paul's use of this text in Rom 15:12). These images are further utilized in Jer 11:10; 23:5; 33:15; Zech 3:8.

6. See Sailhamer, *Meaning of the Pentateuch*, 461.

8

Life Between the Advents
Lord, Where Are You Going?

> Simon Peter said to him, "Lord, where are you going?" Jesus answered him, "Where I am going you cannot follow me now, but you will follow afterward" (Jn 13:36).
>
> Thomas said to him, "Lord, we do not know where you are going. How can we know the way?" (Jn 14:5).

Biblical theology not only strives to see the "big picture" of the grand storyline of Scripture, it also aims to help us see the significance of the "little picture" of our own lives. How do these biblical-theological trajectories intersect with where we are right now in redemptive history?

Christ has come.

Christ will come again.

Nestled into the temporal space between these two confessions, Christians seek to live *this* day in light of *that* Day! Biblical theology can help us navigate life between the Advents: holding fast to our confession and awaiting our blessed hope.

In particular, the resurrection of Christ and the indwelling of the Holy Spirit are two biblical-theological lifelines for us to hold on to as we strive to glorify God and persevere by faith in an oftentimes weary world.

Resurrection Life and the Easter Wager

Everything rides on the reality of resurrection.

A general belief in the resurrection at the end of days is present in the OT. For example, at the end of Daniel's visions, there is a scene that seems very familiar to readers of the book of Revelation. In this scene, "there shall be a time of trouble, such as never has been since there was a nation till that time. But at that time your people shall be delivered, everyone whose name shall be found written in the book" (Dan 12:1). After this, "many of those who sleep in the dust of the earth shall awake, some to everlasting life, and some to shame and everlasting contempt" (Dan 12:2).

This vision affirms a belief in a general resurrection of all those who have died. The vision also affirms that there is to be some sort of judgment following the resurrection. Some will awake to glory, others to terror.

In the Gospels, Jesus also affirms the reality of a future resurrection. He also indicates his role in that resurrection. Jesus tells the crowds, "And this is the will of him who sent me, that I should lose nothing of all that he has given me, but raise it up on the last day" (Jn 6:39). Jesus explains, "For this is the will of my Father, that everyone who looks on the Son and believes in him should have eternal life, and I will raise him up on the last day" (Jn 6:40).

The belief in a general resurrection is given a specific profile by Jesus. Those who believe in the Son will not only awake, but they will awake in his presence.

Everything rides on the reality of resurrection.

One might ask, though, does Jesus really have this kind of power? Can this one really raise the dead at the end of days? The disciples might have asked this very question when Jesus tells them, "Our friend Lazarus has fallen asleep, but I go to awaken him" (Jn 11:11). They don't understand and think Jesus has misjudged the situation. He couldn't really mean that he was going to reverse the sting of death, could he?

Standing outside the tomb of Lazarus, Jesus pictures this resurrection reality with a call that cuts through the complicated layers of doubt: "Lazarus, Come Out!" (Jn 11:43).

Just before this, Martha too had misunderstood. When Jesus said to her, "Your brother will rise again," Martha thinks he is referring to the resurrection hope at the end of days. She says, "I know that he will rise again in the resurrection on the last day" (Jn 11:24). Martha was right. She was simply unaware that Jesus was about to demonstrate the reality of what will take place on *that* day by putting on a display of resurrection life on *this* day.

Her brother would rise again at the end of days, but he would also stand by her side again by the end of this day. To all those who would doubt that he has the power to bring about the resurrection on the last day, Jesus's words breathe hope: "I am the resurrection and the life. Whoever believes in me, though he die, yet shall he live, and everyone who lives and believes in me shall never die" (Jn 11:26).

Paul's gospel message includes this staggering hope in the resurrection. For him, the entire structure of our salvation in Christ rests on the reality of this reality. As he urges, "If there is no resurrection of the dead, then not even Christ has been raised. And if Christ has not been raised, then our preaching is in vain and your faith is in vain" (1 Cor 15:13). Paul insists on the necessity of the resurrection (1 Cor 15:12–28) even while recognizing the mystery of the resurrection (1 Cor 15:50–57).

This is the Easter wager.

If Christ has not been raised, then Christian faith is futile, believers are still stuck in their sin, and those who have died lie in those graves devoid of hope. If the dead are not raised, our blessed hope is six feet under.

"But in fact," Paul counters, "Christ has been raised from the dead" (1 Cor 15:20). This fact means that he is the "firstfruits of those who have fallen asleep. For as by a man came death, by a man has come also the resurrection of the dead" (1 Cor 15:21).

At this point, Paul turns his gaze toward the further up and further in horizon of eschatology. Because Christ rose from the grave, he can now return from the heavens. "Then comes the end," Paul continues, "when he delivers the kingdom to God the Father after destroying every rule and every authority and power" (1 Cor 15:25–26).

Do you grieve for those who have died trusting in Christ to save them? They're gone. We can't see them. Their faith is now out of sight. We're not able to hear them cling to promises and hold on to this resurrection hope. We can no longer overhear them speak, pray, or worship. In that relational silence, our hearts inquire: Was their hope in vain? How can we know for sure if we can no longer see them? Will they really rise on that last day?

Paul tells Thessalonian believers who wondered these very things, "We do not want you to be uninformed, brothers, about those who are asleep, that you may not grieve as others do who have no hope. For since we believe that Jesus died and rose again, even so, through Jesus, God will bring with him those who have fallen asleep. . . . The dead in Christ will rise" (1 Thess 4:13–16).

Everything rides on the reality of resurrection.

As Jesus asked standing in front of a Jewish tomb moments before he stuck a dagger through the heart of death, "Do you believe?"

Ordinary Time and the Pentecost Imperative

What are we supposed to do now?

In the church calendar, there's a clear emphasis on the Christmas season and Easter season. These times are also marked by seasons of preparation. Advent prepares for the celebration of the birth of Christ. Lent prepares for the celebration of the resurrection of Christ.

These two seasons are the anchors of the church's liturgical year. The heart of the gospel is communicated in these times of remembrance.

As Paul remarks in 1 Tim 3:16, "Great indeed, we confess, is the mystery of godliness: He was manifested in the flesh, vindicated by the Spirit, seen by angels, proclaimed among the nations, believed on in the world, taken up in glory."

But what about the times in-between?

After Easter comes Pentecost. After Jesus ascends to the Father's right hand, the Spirit descends upon the gathered believers, indwells them, and inaugurates the new covenant era of redemptive history.

The longest span of time in the liturgical year occurs in the weeks after Pentecost. This season continues all the way through the summer until right before the Advent season begins. This lengthy sequence of weeks is sometimes known as "Ordinary Time."

It's called ordinary time because this season is simply marked by the passing of each week after Pentecost. The numbers are "ordinals" like first, second, third. So, the first Sunday after Pentecost; the second Sunday after Pentecost, and so on.

And on, and on, and on.

So that's why it's called ordinary time; but the possibility of associating this season with the common English connotation of the word "ordinary" is an ever-present temptation that often proves irresistible.

This is the season where nothing happens—the long wilderness between the seasons of celebration; the drought that dehydrates and drains your energy like the grueling halfway point of a long hike in the middle of a blistering summer day.

In ordinary time, nothing changes. It's the same, day after day after day—common; ordinary; unremarkable.

If you are going to make it through the year and persevere to the end, you'll have to learn how to live through ordinary time.

* * *

William Carey was a Baptist missionary from England in the eighteenth century. During a sea voyage on one of his missionary journeys, Carey wrote this in his journal:

"Still sick, -in the Bay of Biscay - Lat. 47 N. Long. 3 W."

One of the reasons Carey kept the journal was to keep his supporters back home informed of his mission work during his trip to India. In the previous entry for June 14, Carey grimly recounts, "Sick, as were all my family and incapable of much reflection." The next day, on June 15, the effect lingers, "Still sick," followed by the latitude and longitude. All Carey records is where he's at and how he feels. The entry itself is sparse, unglamorous, and strikingly unremarkable.

No, "Though my physical body grows sick of the sea with each tumult of this billowing ocean, my soul sallies forth on the waves of supernal bliss as I sojourn to the mission field on celestial wings fueled by the verve of my Spirit-wrought blood-earnestness . . ." Not even a, "You call me out upon the waters . . ."

Just, "Still sick."

A few days later, an entry reads, "Nothing remarkable."

If you've been in ministry for any length of time, you've likely had more than one "still sick in the bay of Biscay" type of day. The minister or missionary must be fueled by more than the *thrill* of adventure when the only thing on the horizon is the *chill* of illness or a long string of unremarkable days.

If we could see Joseph's journal entry about a decade into his imprisonment in Egypt, it might read, "Still wrongly accused and misunderstood. Still in prison." Centuries later, an apostle under house arrest might have recorded on his parchment sometime after his third denied request, "Thorn still in place. Still hurts." Sunburnt and weary, a Jewish carpenter waiting and wandering in a Judean wilderness might have written, "Day 39. Still hungry. Nothing remarkable." Before Jesus faces the devil on day 40, he endures the drudgery of day 39.

In his second letter to the Thessalonians, Paul connects the task of living out the gospel to the work of making a living. Paul and his co-workers were not idle among them, but "with toil and labor" they "worked night and day" so that they would not be a burden (2 Thess 3:8). They even reasoned, "If anyone is not willing to work, let him not eat" (3:10). Some among them were walking in idleness, "not busy at work, but busybodies" (3:11). Paul strongly encourages them "in the Lord Jesus Christ to do their work quietly and to earn their own living" (3:12).

After this specific admonition, Paul backs up and gives a general application. He urges, "Do not grow weary in doing good" (3:13). Fittingly, then, Paul begins his conclusion to the letter by saying, "Now may the Lord of peace himself give you peace at all times in every way. The Lord be with you all" (3:16).

The believer who toils and labors, who works quietly and earns a living, and who does not grow weary in doing good is able to do so precisely because of the promise of the Lord's continuing presence in those moments. Union with Christ means the Lord of peace remains present in your joy, in your pain, in your liftoffs, and in your layovers.

The Christian life is exhilarating. But every journey includes the trial of transit, and sometimes those lulls can make you seasick. The glories of the gospel oftentimes (perhaps most of the time) are proclaimed in the throes of weakness and within the steady rhythms of the unremarkable.

The gospel is not only big enough to leap the gap between departures and destinations; it's also able to settle into the strain of the mundane.

One of the lifelines for the believer who is "in it for the long haul" is the confidence that the God of this gospel grants perseverance in the Christian life even when you're still sick and there's nothing remarkable to report.

* * *

Returning to the rhythm of the church's calendar, the same structure that created the long season of "ordinary time" is also the structure that infuses it with meaning.

Common time is electrified by the two poles that bookend this lengthy season: Pentecost and Advent, the coming of the Spirit and the advent of the incarnation. Indeed, the missions of the Son and the Spirit are the means by which the churches make their way in this world until the end of days.

In the first sermon in the book of Acts, Peter explains that "this Jesus God raised up again, to which we are all witnesses. Therefore having been exalted to the right hand of God, and having received from the Father the promise of the Holy Spirit, He has poured forth this which you both see and hear" (Acts 2:32–33).

The resurrection and the ascension of the Son of God are followed by the outpouring and indwelling of the Spirit of God.

The Easter wager gives way the Pentecost imperative.

The believer who has staked everything on the reality of the resurrection is not left with nothing to do in the new covenant but is given a life-giving command: *Walk in the Spirit.*

Paul makes this type of connection in Rom 6:3–11. He asks, "Do you not know that all of us who have been baptized into Christ Jesus were baptized into his death? We were buried therefore with him by baptism into death, in order that, just as Christ was raised from the dead by the glory of the Father, we too might walk in newness of life."

Paul then reflects on the extraordinary implications of this new walk of life: "For if we have been united with him in a death like his, we shall certainly be united with him in a resurrection like his. We know that our old self was crucified with him in order that the body of sin might be brought to nothing, so that we would no longer be enslaved to sin. For one who has died has been set free from sin."

Freed from the power of sin, Paul drives home the personal and Christological connection: "Now if we have died with

Christ, we believe that we will also live with him. We know that Christ, being raised from the dead, will never die again; death no longer has dominion over him. For the death he died he died to sin, once for all, but the life he lives he lives to God."

Paul's conclusion to this part of his argument is sobering and life-giving. He insists that you "must consider yourselves dead to sin and alive to God in Christ Jesus."

In Rom 8, Paul also writes, "For God has done what the law, weakened by the flesh, could not do. By sending his own Son in the likeness of sinful flesh and for sin, he condemned sin in the flesh, in order that the righteous requirement of the law might be fulfilled in us, who walk not according to the flesh but according to the Spirit" (Rom 8:3–4).

Paul later asserts that "all who are led by the Spirit of God are sons of God. For you did not receive the spirit of slavery to fall back into fear, but you have received the Spirit of adoption as sons, by whom we cry, "Abba! Father!" The Spirit himself bears witness with our spirit that we are children of God, and if children, then heirs—heirs of God and fellow heirs with Christ, provided we suffer with him in order that we may also be glorified with him" (Rom 8:14–17).

This is the Pentecost imperative: *to walk in the Spirit in the newness of life until the Son comes on the clouds and makes all things new.*

A life oriented to the Father, through the Son, and in the Spirit is the believer's goal as the weeks of ordinary time roll on.

As it turns out, ordinary time is where we live most of our lives.

In ordinary time, we live in the electrifying dynamic of the already, the not yet, and the almost.

In ordinary time, we run with endurance the race that is set before us, and we rest in the finished work of the one who has gone before us.

In ordinary time, we work out our salvation with fear and trembling, and we wait with broken hearts and sober joyfulness.

Ordinary time teaches us to endure hardship as discipline, for God is dealing with us as sons.

Ordinary time teaches us about the depth of grace and the rhythm of lament.

In ordinary time, we cling to the promise that "he is risen," that he sat down at the right hand of the majesty on high, that he intercedes for us, and that he is coming quickly.

In ordinary time, we are in it for the long haul and we await our blessed hope.

In Eph 5, Paul gives a charge that is fitting for those who are contemplating their purpose in ordinary time. He urges his readers:

"Pay careful attention, then, to how you walk—not as unwise people but as wise—making the most of the time, because the days are evil. So don't be foolish, but understand what the Lord's will is. And don't get drunk with wine, which leads to reckless living, but be filled by the Spirit: speaking to one another in psalms, hymns, and spiritual songs, singing and making music with your heart to the Lord, giving thanks always for everything to God the Father in the name of our Lord Jesus Christ, submitting to one another in the fear of Christ" (Eph 5:15–21).

If you are alive in this moment, your life matters, and God is calling you to faithfulness in season and out of season.

Ordinary time is a gift.

Discussion & Reflection:

1. Think of a time that you were forced to enter a season of waiting. What are some of the ways you sought to persevere through these "ordinary" times?

2. In 1 Cor 15, why is Paul so adamant about belief in the resurrection?

3. In his letter to the Romans, Paul spends quite a bit of time talking about what it means to "walk in the Spirit." For Paul, what does it look like to walk in the Spirit in this way? How might this emphasis on the Spirit relate to the hope of resurrection and Paul's reminder to "make the most of the time" in our daily lives?

9

Death Between the Advents
How Long, O Lord?

"Until death, mourning and cheerfulness" (Paul Ricoeur).

"As sorrowful, yet always rejoicing" (2 Cor 6:10).

In Shakespeare's play, *Hamlet*, the first time you meet Hamlet himself he is being asked a question by King Claudius. The king inquires, "How is it that the clouds still hang on you?" Hamlet is still grieving the death of his father who had died two months prior. The new king wants Hamlet to move on. In the play, this scenario is connected to all kinds of intrigue, but I have often thought of this question when contemplating the nature of grief.

Does grief have an expiration date? If you have ever grieved in a community, you may have felt the pressure of these questions approach at some point (at first far off, but then increasingly closer): "How is it that the clouds still hang on you?" "Why is your soul still downcast?" "Isn't it time to move on?"

Should we remember the dead? How often? In what way? What about death itself? Is it something we should be mindful of but not meditate on? Aside from specific loss, does talk of death have a place in the Christian community? When we do talk about death and the memory of death in the Christian community, what should guide us?

In the last chapter, we discussed how biblical theology helps us navigate the theological dynamic that comes with living between the Advents of Christ. We already experience the blessings of the new covenant and genuinely have life with God through union with Christ. But we are not yet able to experience the ultimate consummation of God's purposes for the world.

Studying the Bible's meaning and reflecting on its ultimate message equip us to persevere with joy during "ordinary time," and it also provides the means by which we might persevere till the end.

A biblical-theological profile of death, grief, and lament may seem like an overly somber string of notes on which to end our study of biblical theology. But the song of hope that Christ enables us to sing as we live between the Advents requires a minor key in order for it to be rooted in the lives we actually experience.

The Memory of Death as a Theme in Biblical Texts

In Ps 39, the psalmist provides an extended reflection on the limited nature of human existence in the context of guarding himself from sin and thinking rightly about God's character. The psalmist declares, "O Lord, make me know my end and what is the measure of my days" (39:4). Drawing out the implication of this request, he continues, "let me know how fleeting I am!" (39:4).

The psalmist then connects this prayer to an articulation of God's revealed truth about the human condition. "Behold," he says, "you have made my days a few handbreadths, and my lifetime is as nothing before you" (39:5). Because of this reality, "all mankind stands as a mere breath!" and humans live their lives "as a shadow!" (39:5–6).

Later in the psalm, the psalmist exclaims again, "Surely all mankind is a mere breath!" (39:11). Undergirding his plea for the Lord's mercy is that, in contrast to the Lord's permanence, the psalmist is "a sojourner" with the Lord and "a guest" like the rest of humanity (39:12). As the psalmist strives to persevere and contemplate his temporary life, his departure remains in view.

Similarly, in Ps 90, the psalmist contemplates the nature of God who is "from everlasting to everlasting" and compares him to humanity who will inevitably hear the Lord say, "Return, O children of men" to the dust of the earth (Ps 90:3). After noting the relatively limited timespan of even lengthy lives, the psalmist writes, "So teach us to number our days, that we may present to you a heart of wisdom."

Within the flow of this psalm, the phrase "teach us to number our days" is found in a section designed to invite readers to contemplate their mortality and consider that death is assuredly on its way (see also Ps 78:39; Ps 102:23–27).

By speaking in this manner, these psalmists locate the reader within the textual world of the Bible. The creation narrative that begins the biblical storyline grounds human reflection on the nature of humanity. From the dust of the earth, God formed human life (Gen 1–2). Subsequent reflections on returning to the dust draw upon this narrative portrayal of God's creative activity. This allusion to dust as a way to demonstrate the inevitability and finality of death is a powerful intertextual image. If this connection is true, there is no escape from either death or the dust.

The book of Ecclesiastes begins with the preacher's declaration, "Vanity of vanities! All is vanity" (Eccl 1:2). "What does man gain," the preacher asks, "from all the toil at which he toils under the sun?" (1:3). The inevitability of death informs this question: "A generation goes, and a generation comes, but the earth remains forever" (1:4).

At the end of the book, the preacher returns to this theme by urging, "Remember also your Creator in the days of your youth, before the evil days come and the years draw near of which you will say, 'I have no pleasure in them'" (12:1).

After a poetic description of the aging process, the preacher concludes "the dust returns to the earth as it was, and the spirit returns to God who gave it" (12:7). "Vanity of vanities," the preacher repeats, "all is vanity" (12:8). Though the message of Ecclesiastes relates to the book's final call to "fear God and keep his commandments, for this is the whole duty of man" (12:13), these echoes of the Genesis creation accounts prompt a searching reflection on human mortality even for those who ultimately find meaning in obedience to God's will.

In his NT epistle, James also speaks about the inevitably brief human lifespan when considered in light of eternity. James writes, "Come now, you who say, 'Today or tomorrow we will go to such and such a city and spend a year there and engage in business and make a profit.' Yet you do not know what your life will be like tomorrow. You are just a vapor that appears for a little while and then vanishes away. Instead, you ought to say, 'If the Lord wills, we will live and also do this or that'" (Jas 4:13–15).

This poetic word picture communicates both presence and transience. The presence of the vapor is real but momentary, established but ephemeral, present but in the process of passing away. For James, an ongoing dependence on the Lord and perspective on life with the proper amount of humility is engendered by reflecting upon the uncertainty of the future, the inevitability of death, and the impermanence of human existence in relation to God's existence.

The exhortations in these biblical passages ("teach us") show that the theme of death is connected to the present function of the memory of death for the believer ("to number our days"). Remembering both the dust of your past and the dust of your future enables you to reorient the drawn breaths of your present.

Of course, in each of these contexts there is a broader discourse at work that connects these reminders of human mortality with broader theological purposes. However, the point here is that this theme is utilized directly by biblical writers and connected to theological reflection upon the human condition.

The Memory of Death as a Theme in Church History

This theme of remembering death surfaces directly at various points in the history of the church as well. There are many ways to highlight this topic, so we will focus here on a few ways that reflection on death appears in different times and in different mediums.

The phrase *memento mori* ("remember death") is sometimes used to describe this movement in artistic depictions of objects, like a skull, that were designed to remind the viewer of the ever-present reality of death. A complementary concept to *memento mori* is the *vanitas* theme in art in the seventeenth century and beyond. This theme draws upon the phrase "vanity of vanities" from Ecclesiastes and seeks to illustrate the transitory nature of life and also the meaninglessness of material possessions as an end in themselves.

This theme can be seen in the still life portraits produced in Europe in the fifteenth through seventeenth centuries. These paintings included objects that visually reminded viewers of death (a skull), the inevitability of future loss of life (a plucked flower), the pervasive presence of present loss (an extinguished candle), the inexorable passage of time (an hourglass), or the fleeting nature of one's life (bubbles in the air).[1]

This emphasis can also be found in the writings of pastors and theologians. For example, among the Puritans, there was often an emphasis on remembering death as a means of developing in Christian maturity and the hope of the resurrection. Related to the theme of "remembering death" (*memento mori*) is the notion of the "art of dying" or "dying well" (*ars moriendi*). This impulse showed up in tombstones, woodcuts, treatises, and sermons.

For example, a tombstone in this period reads, "Death which came on man by the fall / cuts down father child and all."[2] A characteristic example of these exhortations can be seen in Cotton Mather's reminder that his readers will "die shortly." He therefore urges, "Let us look upon everything as a sort of Death's Head set before us, with a *memento mortis* written upon it."[3]

In many ways, our contemporary cultural mindset neglects or outright rejects this "reminder of death" as a valued component of everyday life. Much of our celebrity culture and current social context is designed to mute our sense of mortality, to make us less mindful about the looming specter of death, the inevitability of age, and the reality of our finitude.

An enduring strand of contemporary culture seeks to produce, market, and monetize products and approaches to life that fixate on making you look and feel young and project an image of the good life that obviously does not include sober reflection on mortality.[4]

Recognizing the inherent value of healthy living patterns, some of these approaches pursue these ends as a therapeutic tool to also engender a psychological well-being that seeks to slow the path to death at all costs and mask the appearance of age. Collectively, these orienting practices function as "some of the most important and powerful cultural myths of our day."[5]

In these cases, rituals of remembrance are replaced by a liturgy of forgetfulness.

This contemporary avoidance of reflection on death is sometimes shared by Christian communities. Certainly, this is in part because of the influence of a general cultural mindset that often avoids talk of death. However, within the Christian community, often a focus on the reality of death and suffering is eclipsed by an understandable focus on the hope of the gospel, future glory, and the believer's pursuit of faith-filled trust in the Lord.

These two features, though, sometimes create a church culture that leaves only a limited amount of "space" for the memory of death, the articulation of grief, and the vagaries of lived-out suffering over long periods of time.

This leads many in the churches to ask directly: Is an awareness of death (*memento mori*) in general and lament more specifically appropriate in the Christian life and as a feature of corporate worship?

Death reaches every corner of life, is constantly around us, and is inescapable. If our theology cannot handle death, it's not worth believing.

The Christian Response of Biblical Lament

One reason the Christian community should provide a space to grieve for believers and unbelievers around us is because this process is a necessary element of the human condition. A deeper reason is because within the context of the Scriptures and the Christian community, there are already deeply integrated resources that can guide and govern the task of remembering death and practicing lament in personal, corporate, and public life.

What does it take to Lament?
Time, Space, and Training

What would it take in order to remember death and practice lament in personal and corporate Christian settings? Three components seem to be necessary: physical time, conceptual space, and theological training.

A quick word about each: *Physical time* is required in order for this type of thoughtful reflection to take place. The passing of time is often necessary to even begin to process the full scope of a given experience. This extended period of reflection also needs *conceptual space* to explore the gravity of death, to actually experience grief in its full-bodied expression, and then be able to connect it to the nature of life and the hope of the gospel. Finally, a believer needs *theological training* that communicates the freedom to explore both the horror of human pain and the hope of the gospel in that same conceptual space.

In practice, sometimes the Christian community has offered counsel or encouragement to grieving people without the time or space required to process grief and the memory of death. This sometimes manifests as hastily spoken cultural clichés (like, "time heals all wounds") or well-intentioned biblical phrases that stand in for meta-explanations for all pain and this pain in particular ("all things happen for a reason," "All things work together for good").

While phrases spoken in these moments have varying levels of helpfulness (and truthfulness in some cases), in light of our discussion here, what oftentimes renders these sentiments ineffective (and perhaps offensive in some instances) is that they are delivered apart from a conceptual space that also affirms the full-bodied affirmation and validation of someone's feeling of loss.

They only put a band-aid on our brokenness.

We may need to shift the metaphors: Something is not only slightly out of place; something is gone. A limb has been lost. It's helpful sometimes to rush to a new situation with ways to stop the bleeding. But after the bleeding stops, you have to learn how to walk again without that limb. While they serve a temporary purpose, well-meaning band-aids are not capable of helping heal wounds that last a lifetime.

Exploring the Rhythm of Biblical Lament

Lament in biblical literature is predominantly found in poetic form. One of the effects of poetry is that it is designed to slow readers down and force them to consider the relationship between sentences, lines, words, images, and metaphors. Most biblical poetry is also either found within collections of poetry or embedded within larger narratives.

In both of these canonical contexts, readers are asked to make sense of lament in light of a broader assortment of theological and textual realities. As a reader of the Psalter, for instance, you will read Ps 23's "the Lord is my shepherd I shall not want" alongside Ps 22's "My God, my God, why have you forsaken me?"

If we take the arrangement of the Psalter seriously and seek to accept its interpretive guidance as we read and reread it as a complex compositional whole, one of the questions that will continually confront us is this: How do soaring expressions of praise and worship relate to sinking articulations of sorrow? What about when they stand side by side in the Psalter? What about when they stand side by side within the same psalm? What about when they reside side by side within the same reader of those psalms?

Another example is the phrase, "His mercies never come to an end; they are new every morning," which is often utilized in times of suffering. Consider, though, its textual location in the book of Lamentations as a whole and its canonical location within the Writings of the Hebrew Bible.

Lam 3:21–42 is indeed a soaringly beautiful and deeply comforting passage of Scripture. However, it is set within a book-length lament that begins in chapter 1, "How lonely sits the city that was full of people! How like a widow she has become, she who was great among the nations! . . . She weeps bitterly in the night with tears on her cheeks," and ends in chapter 5 with phrases like, "The joy of our hearts has ceased; our dancing has been turned to mourning. . . . Why do you forget us forever; why do you forsake us for so many days?"

The final words of the book are a plea, "Restore us to yourself, O Lord, that we may be restored! Renew our days as of old — unless you have utterly rejected us, and you remain exceedingly angry with us" (5:21–22).

The textual location of the phrase, "His mercies never come to an end," then, forces the reader of the book of Lamentations to consider the relationship between articulations of pain and grief from loss of life and sorrow over acknowledged sin and the hope of enduring mercy from the Lord. The genre of lament provides both physical time (the actual reading of a book and the processing of poetic images) and conceptual space for a reader (both types of theological affirmations being present).

In some of Paul's letters, the relationship between death and life is at the center of his discussion of persevering through suffering. For example, in 2 Cor 4, he speaks of having the treasure of the gospel in "earthen vessels, so that the surpassing greatness of the power will be of God and not from ourselves" (4:7). He continues with a string of unexpected juxtapositions: "we are afflicted in every way, but not crushed; perplexed, but not despairing; persecuted, but not forsaken; struck down, but not destroyed; always carrying about in the body the dying of Jesus, so that the life of Jesus also may be manifested in our body" (4:8-9).

These statements are obviously connected to the argument Paul is making in this section of his letter, but the point here is that Paul seems to be homing in on this dynamic of the continual presence of some form of suffering, the given of human frailty, and simultaneously the ongoing certainty of gospel truth.

Life is finite. The body is decaying. Death is coming. But God's life is infinite. Salvation in Christ is real and connects us to that hope even now. To our point here, Paul extends this dynamic through to the next chapter's discussion of "the earthly tent," which will be torn down and in which we currently groan (2 Cor 5:1–10). He seems to be describing not only a temporary state of affairs but rather an element of the human condition that any articulation of hope must take into account.

In a similar vein in Rom 8, Paul declares that nothing will separate us from the love of God in Christ and immediately connects this assertion to the statement that "we are being put to death all day long" (8:36).

Our Pain and the Hope of Glory

Finally, the biblical storyline as a whole that is envisioned at the end of Isaiah and the end of the Revelation seems to draw together a vision of paradise restored alongside of a sober acknowledgement of the suffering that always marks life on earth between Eden and the New Jerusalem (Isa 65–66; Rev 21–22).

As the voice from heaven says in Rev 21, "He will wipe away every tear from their eyes; and there will no longer be any death; there will no longer be any mourning, or crying, or pain; the first things have passed away" (21:5). On *that* day, tears will be wiped away. On *this* day, they continue to flow forth.

These are just a few examples of the way biblical texts closely draw together full acknowledgements of human suffering with certain conviction of gospel hope. We could add more, and there is certainly more to say about these passages. However, these illustrate the theme at hand.

These textual and canonical features are important resources in creating time and space for lament in the Christian community. The biblical-theological themes of the certainty of death and the certainty of hope sit side by side within these textual locations by design.

Because biblical lament contains and connects both of these themes, we should continue to consider new ways to allow lament to guide and govern our response to a world teeming with both life and death.

In other words, the Christian community rightly emphasizes that believers grieve, but not as those without hope.

Sometimes, though, we might need to be reminded that until he comes, we hope, but not as those without grief.

Discussion & Reflection:

1. Have you noticed any ways that our culture works to avoid any talk of death? What is a clear example of this tendency? Can you think of any cultural exceptions to this pattern?

2. Have you thought much about the concept of biblical lament? More than 1/3 of the psalms in the Book of Psalms could be categorized as a "psalm of lament." Read Ps 42 and describe the different kinds of affirmations and emotions that sit side by side in this poetic text.

3. Does it feel fitting to incorporate biblical lament in your normal routine of worship and devotion? Does something feel off about doing this? Would your answer change depending on the situation or context? (for example: during a season of suffering vs. during a time of personal peace, or during personal devotion vs. during corporate gatherings).

Notes:

1. A famous example of this is by Philippe de Champaigne, a Belgium artist living in France, who produced "Still-life with a skull" (1671), which features a close-up of a simple table with three objects side-by-side: a skull in the center, a recently picked tulip in a vase on the left, and an emptying hourglass on the right.

2. Cited in Stannard, "Death and Dying," 1313. Cf. Roark, *Artists of Colonial America*, who notes that "the most common inscriptions on Puritan gravestones prior to about 1710 are the Latin 'fugit hora' (time flies) and 'memento mori,' which translated means 'remember death' but also refers to the popular epitaph, 'As you are now, so once was I; as I am now you soon shall be. Remember death and follow me'" (60).

3. Cotton Mather, *Death Made Easie & Happy* (London, 1701), 94. For an extended discussion of this historical section (and the rest of this chapter), see Spellman, "What Remains of Our Lament?" in *SWJT* (2019): 127–49. The *memento mori* theme among the Puritans (and others in church history) was not always positive or theologically constructive. The big idea for this chapter, though, is that the pervasive presence of these works demonstrates the long history of literary and theological reflection on death and the function that a memory of death has for the meaning of life.

4. For a brief overview of some of the historical factors that have led to this scenario and an analysis of some of the possible effects of this cultural situation, see the orienting discussion in McCullough, *Remember Death*, 31–56.

5. See Vanhoozer's exploration of "the well-documented North American obsession with the health, fitness, and well-being of our physical bodies" in *Hearers and Doers*, 13–42.

10

Your Story and His Story
Biblical Theology as a Way of Life

There comes a moment when the children who have been playing at burglars hush suddenly: was that a *real* footstep in the hall? There comes a moment when people who have been dabbling in religion suddenly draw back. Supposing we really found Him? We never meant it to come to *that*! Worse still, supposing He had found us? (C.S. Lewis, *Miracles*).

So Philip ran to him and heard him reading Isaiah the prophet and asked, "Do you understand what you are reading?" And he said, "How can I, unless someone guides me?" (Acts 8:30–31).

Jesus answered . . . "Everyone who is of the truth listens to my voice." Pilate said to him, "What is truth?" (Jn 18:37–38).

In the late 1900s, we had these cultural and economic centers of social life called "malls." Though you can certainly find them today, they no longer function as the go-to nexus of entertainment and interpersonal opportunity for the youths of our digitally networked societal ecosystem.

Coming of age in America's community Mall era, a trip to this location was serious business. Because there were so many stores packed together, it was important to know which direction you needed to head while you navigated the oversized shopping bags of passing people and the roving groups of angsty teenagers (for me, finding the trading card shop or the bookstore while avoiding the fog of perfume creeping out from the entrance of JC Penney!).

Because the flip phone was not yet capable of navigational assistance, in each entrance there were giant directory signs that showed a map layout of each section of the mall. Usually, there was also a big red arrow that helped you orient yourself to where you were with the words "YOU ARE HERE."

As a teenaged introvert in the 90s looking for the bookstore in the local mall, these signs were both welcome and helpful.

As a believer trying to make my way through the world, a sign that tells me where I'm located in God's plan for my life, in the scope of redemptive history, and in relation to the crowds of competing voices vying for my attention and devotion is both urgent and essential.

In his grace and providence, God has given us this kind of guidance in a wide-ranging collection of sacred Scripture. One of the best ways to deepen your understanding of this canonical collection and tune your ears to hear what the Spirit is saying through these words is the discipline of biblical theology.

* * *

The overall aim of this little book has been to orient you to this kind of study called "biblical theology" and give you a few ways to think about the message of the Bible as a whole.

The approach taken in this volume focuses on and directly relates the canon, the covenants, and the Christ. The Scriptures were composed, gathered, and circulated in such a way that they are able to communicate God's revelation of his saving message for future generations.

This canonical context, then, is where we encounter the biblical writings. Moreover, a grand storyline arises from the many narratives comprising this canonical collection. The heartbeat of this storyline can be heard in the biblical covenants.

Both the canonical collection and the biblical covenants point to Jesus as the Christ. These three interconnected categories — the canon, the covenants, and the Christ — have structured this attempt to capture the crucial components of biblical theology.

The Master Teacher's Lesson about Himself

In the opening chapter of this book, we looked at Irenaeus's comment about our dependence on God for theological knowledge: "The Lord taught us that no man is capable of knowing God, unless he be taught of God; that is, that God cannot be known without God." This is also an appropriate place to conclude our reflection on biblical theology.

Our approach to biblical theology can be guided by Jesus himself.

The fourfold Gospel serves a special canonical function in its collective portrayal of Jesus as the master teacher. A strong line of textual and theological continuity among the four Gospels is the central place of Jesus's words and the strategic function of his teachings in each narrative.

"In the beginning was the Word," John begins, and the "Word became flesh and dwelt among us" (Jn 1:1, 14). The Word dwelt among us. The Word also *spoke* among us!

In the Gospels we behold his glory by reading and hearing his words.

Matthew incorporates large blocks of Jesus's discourse at strategic locations in his book (e.g., the sermon on the mount in Matt 5–7). Mark typically focuses on Jesus's actions, but he also highlights a block of Jesus's parables on the kingdom (Mk 4) and discussion of the end of days (Mk 13).

Luke's extensive account of Jesus's final journey to Jerusalem is dominated by teaching, parables, and proclamations on the cost and treasure of discipleship (Lk 1–9). John provides lengthy accounts of Jesus's theological conversations and mega-prayers (Jn 14–17).

In these ways, all the Gospel writers strategically showcase the fact that Jesus is a master teacher whose words embody divine wisdom and carry unparalleled weight. Jesus as a master teacher, then, represents both a common theological theme in the Gospels and a clear facet of each writer's compositional strategy.

Jesus brings out of the storehouses words old and new (Matt 13:52) as he *fulfills* and *fills out* messianic expectation. Common refrains in the Gospels include, "Whose son is he?" and, "Who is this man?"

Many answers are given to these questions, but the burden of the Gospel writers is to show that Jesus provides the definitive answer to these questions he himself often raises.

One of the convictions of a confessional approach to reading the Bible is that through these words this same Christ beckons us as readers, "What about you? Who do you say that I am?"

The First and Last Words of the Resurrected Christ

The confession of the apostles and earliest churches was that an emphasis on living the "quoted life" as readers and re-readers of the Scriptures is modeled after the example of the risen Christ himself.

Indeed, our first and final glimpses of Jesus after the resurrection show him testifying about the work of God in the world on the basis of the Scriptures.

Remarkably, according to Luke's Gospel, the first theologian of the death, resurrection, and ongoing ministry of the Messiah is the risen Christ in the dawn of resurrection Sunday. In other words, the first one to produce a post-resurrection "biblical theology of the Messiah" is the resurrected Christ himself.

As he journeys *toward* Jerusalem before the cross, Jesus explains that "the son of man must suffer many things . . . and be killed, and on the third day be raised" (Lk 9:22). As he journeys *away* from Jerusalem after the resurrection, he continues to help his disciples connect his own person and work to the big picture of the Bible.

On the road to Emmaus with his down-trodden disciples, Jesus leads them on a path through the Scriptures. "Beginning with Moses and all the Prophets," Luke recounts, Jesus "interpreted to them in all the Scriptures the things concerning himself" (Lk 24:27). This scriptural exposition across the OT canon is prompted by questions about the meaning of the Messiah's mission: "Wasn't it necessary for the Messiah to suffer these things and enter into his glory?" (Lk 24:26).

Appearing later to a larger group of disciples, Jesus reiterates, "These are my words that I spoke to you while I was still with you — that everything written about me in the Law of Moses, the Prophets, and the Psalms must be fulfilled" (Lk 24:44). He then "opened their minds to understand the Scriptures" (Lk 24:45). Here we see explicit reference to and interaction with the canonical collection in the context of a message about the progress of redemptive history and the fulfillment of covenantal promises.

* * *

Seen within the context of the Christian canon, Rev 22 serves an exceedingly fitting role in providing closure to the grand storyline of the Bible and also the canonical collection in which that story is told. The gospel of the Gospels, the growth of the churches in Acts and the epistles, and John's culminating vision in Revelation are readily understood to be organically connected because of the unfolding shape of the NT collection. The claim of these biblical texts is that the apostolic message about the past and also the future is sufficient for the believing community in the present until he comes.

The first words of Revelation characterize what follows as the direct communication of Jesus mediated through his messengers to be received by future generations of readers: "The revelation of Jesus Christ, which God gave him to show to his servants the things that must soon take place. He made it known by sending his angel to his servant John, who bore witness to the word of God and to the testimony of Jesus Christ, even to all that he saw" (Rev 1:1–2). Directly connecting the Christian life to the reading of written revelation, John declares, "Blessed is the one who reads aloud the words of this prophecy, and blessed are those who hear, and who keep what is written in it, for the time is near" (Rev 1:1–3).

Jesus's words at the very end of the book match these and anticipate the canonical shape of the NT: "I, Jesus, have sent my angel to testify to you about these things for the churches" (Rev 22:16). In addition to the heavenly vision, this testimony likely includes the letters that Jesus commissioned to be read by the churches (Rev 2–3). These individually addressed letters were then circulated as part of the book of Revelation. Here, then, is a depiction of the risen Christ directly commissioning what becomes in time the culminating entry of the NT collection.

Jesus then joins this apostolic message to an ancient promise about a coming son of David: "I am the Root and descendant of David, the bright morning star" (Rev 22:16). Part of the rhetorical effect of these statements about apostolic testimony and prophetic expectation is that they are the last words of the resurrected Jesus that readers encounter in the NT. This concluding sequence in Revelation encourages readers to remember old textual and theological links even as they reflect upon fresh gospel proclamation.

The first and last words of the risen Christ to the churches have a shared strategy: to give believers hope for the future on the basis of the meaning of biblical texts and the grand storyline of the biblical canon.

Reading and Re-Reading as a Way of Life

When I was in seminary, for several months I met with an older man who was part of a halfway house ministry that helped people transition into the workforce after being homeless or in prison. He had been a believer for a few years, but he had never read much of the Bible.

When I started meeting with him, we read several chapters from John's Gospel each week. As we made our way through the story, he became interested in Peter, so for our next book study he picked Peter's letters. That sounded good to me, so the next week we met to discuss 1 Peter.

When we began talking about the letter, though, an odd thing began to happen. He kept giving a very negative reading of Peter's message and tone in his letter. He would say things like, "Well, Peter is sad in this letter. He's unsure of himself. He doesn't really feel like he has a right to speak to these people."

This line of conversation went on for a few minutes. Confused as to why he was reading this very specific psychological profile into what is a strongly worded and confident letter, I simply asked him why he thought Peter would be thinking these things. He then said, "Well, Peter betrayed Jesus and abandoned him. How could you ever recover from something like that?"

Now I saw the issue more clearly. What had happened was that he was reading Peter's letter in light of only half of

Peter's story. He was familiar with the Gospel narrative of Peter's denial of Jesus, and his last memory of Peter before reading 1 Pet 1:1 was Peter cursing Jesus and the shame and horrifying betrayal exposed by the sound of the rooster's crow.

After realizing that this was where he was coming from, I told him, "Well, that's not the end of Peter's story!" We then returned to the closing chapters of John's Gospel to revisit Peter's restoration with Jesus along the shore, and then briefly surveyed Peter's prominent role in the book of Acts as a confident preacher of the gospel. We saw Peter explain the new covenant, preach to thousands, follow the guidance of the Holy Spirit, shape the direction of the early church, and boldly serve the resurrected Christ.

"Well," he said, "that changes everything. Knowing this about Peter changes how I read his letter for sure!"

* * *

In Acts 17, Paul and Silas arrive in Berea under the cover of night after a serious conflict in Thessalonica. When they arrive, they enter the Jewish synagogue and proclaim the gospel message (Acts 17:10–11). Luke recounts that "these Jews were more noble than those in Thessalonica" because they "received the word with all eagerness, examining the Scriptures daily to see if these things were so" (17:11).

The message the Bereans examine here is likely the same one that Paul preached in Thessalonica. Luke notes that over the course of three Sabbaths in Thessalonica, Paul "reasoned with them from the Scriptures, explaining and proving that it was necessary for the Christ to suffer and to rise from the dead" (17:2–3). Paul explains in his preaching, "This Jesus whom I proclaim to you, is the Christ" (17:3).

These ancient Bereans can be a model for contemporary believers and biblical theologians. A Berean brand of biblical theology argues that the careful study of the whole Bible on its own terms is organically connected to the preaching of the gospel and the ministry of the churches.

The Berean practice of reading the Scriptures in light of the risen Christ can shape both our understanding of the big picture of the Bible and also our exegetical practice.

This scene also illustrates several of the principles developed throughout this volume: The gospel is a story that takes two testaments to tell. The biblical authors were also biblical readers. The task of biblical theology requires reading and rereading. And so on.

The reading and heeding of God's written revelation in the Scriptures is the means by which the churches fulfill the great commission and cling to the promises of Christ until he comes.

The Road to Emmaus and an Army of Artists

"Did not our hearts burn within us while he talked to us on the road, while he opened to us the Scriptures?" (Lk 24:32).

The post-resurrection scene in Luke 24 is a *locus classicus* for the belief that the OT Scriptures testify to the person and work of Jesus as the Christ. As mentioned above, this scene is rife with relevance for the discipline of biblical theology.

Here the risen Christ engages his own disciples about the meaning of his incarnate life, death, and resurrection by referring to the message of the Hebrew Bible as a whole (Lk 24:27, 44). He later appears to them again, clarifies the gospel message that they are being called to proclaim among the nations by the power of the Spirit, and then ascends into the heavens (24:44–53).

Before this, though, Luke allows the scene to linger on Jesus's initial encounter with the two disciples walking along the road to Emmaus. With intense theo-dramatic irony, Jesus prompts them to speak of "all that had happened in Jerusalem" these past few days. This hermeneutical trek through the OT ends as evening descends and they turn in for the night at Emmaus.

As they begin their evening meal, Jesus blesses the bread, breaks it, and hands it to the disciples. At this moment, Luke recounts that "their eyes were opened, and they recognized him" (24:31). In that moment of recognition, Jesus disappears from their sight, and they are left to mull over his words and marvel at his recent presence in their midst.

In addition to biblical studies, this scene has a rich reception history in the world of art. The supper at Emmaus is not the most frequently depicted biblical scene, but it has captured the imagination of some of the most well-known artists across different periods of art history. Several artists also returned to this scene at different stages of their career.

For example, the Italian painter Caravaggio twice envisioned the moment of Christ's revelation of himself to his disciples at the breaking of bread at the table. This is perhaps one of the most famous Emmaus paintings, and it graces the covers of many works of biblical theology (Caravaggio's Emmaus is to biblical theology what Rublev's three visitors are to Trinitarian theology).

In his first painting (*Supper at Emmaus*, 1601), the colors are vibrant, the table meal is fresh and full, and the scene emphasizes the dramatic and discombobulating moment when Jesus's identity dawns on the amazed disciples. Christ is at the center, blessing the bread with one hand and with the other almost reaching out toward the viewer. There is also an open seat at the table that is like a visual invitation to join the scene and consider the identity of Jesus as the resurrected Lord.

In his second painting (*Supper at Emmaus*, 1606), the tone is considerably darkened, the table and meal are much more sparse, and the features of Jesus and the disciples are more rugged and gritty (showing the details of age and almost conveying weariness). Whereas the first seems to emphasize the brilliant shock of the moment, the second draws the viewer into the Christological denouement with a sober and understated approach.

The Dutch Rembrandt also painted this scene multiple times in his lifetime. His first has a simple setting with Jesus's figure on the right side of the canvas being illuminated from behind by candlelight (*Supper at Emmaus*, 1629). One disciple is in the light and leaning away from Christ in shock, and the other is fully in the shadows, bowing at Jesus's feet after falling out of his chair.

About twenty years later, Rembrandt returned to this scene in a more well-known work (*The Supper at Emmaus*, 1648, which now hangs at The Louvre). In this version, the perspective has shifted, and Jesus is now at the center of the table. The room is brighter from window light and a halo-like radiance flows from behind Jesus's head as he begins to break the bread. The table in front of Jesus has also been cleared, and the bright white tablecloth is reminiscent of the ceremonial setting of the Eucharist.

In their repeated treatment of this scene, both of these painters utilize techniques of shadow, light, tone, and color to convey a range of interpretive emphases. Caravaggio shifted from vibrant features to understated elements. Rembrandt moved from a simple atmosphere to an almost sanctuary-like setting.

With these two kinds of depictions, perhaps these artists wanted to explore both the joy and cost of discipleship. Sometimes lavish, sometimes sparse. Feast and famine. The freshness of insight alongside the fatigue of endurance. The revelation of Christ and the realization of the cross. In this sometimes confusing human condition, Christ still beckons you to join him at the table. Taste and see.

The painting that is part of the cover of this little book is another entry in the reception history of this theologically rich table scene. In the middle of his career, Henry Ossawa Tanner (1859–1937) envisioned this scene with similarities to and key differences from the works by other artists (*The Pilgrims at Emmaus*, 1905). Tanner's mother was a former slave, and his father was a minister and abolitionist. He overcame racism that hindered his education as a student and went on to become the first African American artist to gain international acclaim (especially in France). Perhaps from the influence of his father, as he approached middle-age, Tanner rededicated himself to the Christian life and began to focus his art on biblical scenes (some of his most well-known paintings are *The Resurrection of Lazarus*, 1898 and *the Annunciation*, 1898).

In his Emmaus painting, Tanner calls the disciples "pilgrims" and gives the scene a quiet and warm atmosphere. The table is bright white with the bread and a plate of fruit clearly visible. Tanner is known for his experiments with the depiction of light, and here the room is dim with dark shadows beneath the table and around the room. Because Jesus and the two disciples are dressed in dark clothes, the white tablecloth on Jesus's side of the table is particularly bright.

A warm light is emanating from Jesus's face and hands as the scene captures the moment of blessing the bread. Jesus's face is radiant with an uplifted gaze, but you can still see the lines on his face and the scruff of his facial hair. The warm light from Jesus is reflected in the faces of the two disciples, who look as if they are in the seconds directly before identity of the risen Christ dawns on them.

As Caravaggio and Rembrandt had done before him, Tanner memorably illustrates Luke's narrative portrayal of a scene that marks the beginning of a new covenant era of the life of faith and ecclesial fellowship. These artistic attempts to capture the brilliance of Christ's revelation and the shock of its reception among his disciples put the vibrant dynamic of Christian discipleship on full display.

In their central task, biblical theologians are like artists who read and reflect on the meaning of individual passages and the message of the biblical canon as a whole. They then attempt to portray the unchanging truth of this unbreakable word in creative ways that help us see the literary beauty, the theological depth, and the shimmering brilliance of these sacred texts.

This is why the task of biblical theology will last until the end of days and require a great cloud of witnesses. We need sketch artists, casual painters, masters of technique and style, amateurs making stick figures, and children drawing in the sand. We need sidewalk chalk, booths at the bazaar, satellite imagery, drone footage, exhibits in the museum, and formal portraits in the national gallery. However talented and competent a work of art might be, the grand storyline God's work in the world will never be captured by a lone virtuoso.

It requires an army of artists. So join up. Get to work with whatever tools you have. Keep painting your piece in the mosaic of the story God is calling into being.

* * *

In the end, biblical theology helps you navigate *the world of the biblical text* and also helps you locate yourself in *the biblical text's world*.

No better place to be.

Discussion & Reflection

1. Now that we've reached the end (not of all things but of this book!), what has stood out to you most about the task of biblical theology? What would you identify as "new" (things you haven't considered before), and what would you identify as "review" (things you have considered but perhaps not in relation to biblical theology)?

2. What are some of the ways that this approach to biblical theology might inform the life of the churches or your ministry situation in particular?

3. How might the study of biblical theology help you on a personal level as you strive to respond to God's word, discern God's will, and live by faith in your daily life?

Part 2

Where do I go from Here?
Resources for Further Study

Books for Further Reading
What Do I Read From Here?

BT Series:

New Studies in Biblical Theology (IVP); Essential Studies in Biblical Theology (IVP); Short Studies in Biblical Theology (Crossway); Biblical Theology for Life (Zondervan); Studies in Scripture & Biblical Theology (Lexham). Each of these series includes volumes that address method but mostly focus on central themes in BT (either at the level of the whole Bible or a canonical book/sub-collection). The NSBT stands out as a flagship series for the evangelical resurgence of BT in the last few decades. (Introductory/intermediate/advanced)

BT Reference Works:

Alexander, T. Desmond and Brian Rosner, eds. *New Dictionary of Biblical Theology: Exploring the Unity & Diversity of Scripture.* IVP, 1998. Substantive collection of essays on method, BT themes, and a variety of related topics. An excellent first stop for research projects. (Intermediate/advanced)

Beale, G.K., D.A. Carson, Benjamin Gladd, and Andrew Naselli, eds. *Dictionary of the New Testament Use of the Old Testament.* A companion volume to the *Commentary on the NT use of the OT,* serves as a nice complement to the *NDBT* as well. Alongside of NT use of OT, helpfully includes entries on individual books and the OT use of the OT. (Intermediate/advanced)

BT Volumes:

Hafemann, Scott J. *Biblical Theology: Retrospect & Prospect* (IVP, 2002). These essays give a snapshot of the BT discussions at the turn of the century. Still very useful because they address perennial issues like the use of history, the biblical canon, and the nature of biblical composition. (Advanced)

Hamilton, James M. *What is Biblical Theology? A Guide to the Bible's Story, Symbolism, and Patterns.* Crossway, 2013. Brief introduction to Hamilton's approach to BT, which pays close attention to the "interpretive perspective" of the biblical authors and the literary patterns of the text. (Introductory)

Klink, Edward and Darian Lockett. *Understanding Biblical Theology: A Comparison of Theory and Practice.* Zondervan, 2012. Surveys contemporary approaches to BT along a History—Theology spectrum. Excellent tool for understanding the differences between different BT projects. (Introductory/intermediate)

Lawrence, Michael. *Biblical Theology in the Life of the Church: A Guide for Ministry.* Crossway, 2010. Introduces big ideas of BT as a discipline with a focus on practical application. Has a helpfully integrated vision for exegesis, BT, and systematic theology for pastoral ministry. (Introductory/intermediate)

Roark, Nick and Robert Cline. *Biblical Theology: How the Church Faithfully Teaches the Gospel.* Crossway/Nine Marks, 2018. Excellent primer on the task of BT with attention to the Bible's "big story" and its connection to the teaching and mission of the church. (Introductory)

Sailhamer, John. *Introduction to Old Testament Theology: A Canonical Approach.* Zondervan, 1995. While focused on OT theology, Sailhamer addresses BT as a discipline throughout. Because of his careful focus on the hermeneutical choices that inform exegesis and BT, this volume has enduring significance. An excellent place to start an advanced study of the field. (Advanced)

Schreiner, Thomas. *The King in His Beauty: A Biblical Theology of the Old and New Testaments.* Overview of the storyline of the OT & NT with a special emphasis on the BT theme of the Kingdom of God. Includes solidly evangelical treatment of the main message of each biblical book. (Intermediate)

Topics for Further Study
What Do I Research From Here?

In the following pages, I provide these elements for a series of possible research directions: 1) the research topic, 2) a series of starter research questions, 3) several talking points regarding the possible payoff of this research, and 4) a number of solid sources that will help you start your research reading or formal project.

Research Topics

1. **What is Biblical Theology?**
   Defining the Discipline of BT

2. **Biblical Theology and the Biblical Canon**
   Canonical Approaches to BT

3. **The Grand Storyline of the Bible**
   How the Bible is and is not a "Story"

4. **Biblical Theology and the Covenants**
   The Nature and Function of the Biblical Covenants

5. **The "Center" of Biblical Theology**
   Arguments for and against Central Themes

6. **Finding Christ in All of Scripture**
   The Differing Paths to a Christological Reading

7. **Biblical Theology and Interpretive Methods**
   Typology, Allegory, and Intertextuality

8. **Biblical Theology and the Great Tradition**
   Exploring Precursors to the Discipline of BT

1. What is Biblical Theology?
Defining the Discipline of BT

Starter Questions: What is the best way to define the task of BT? Should BT be considered a discrete discipline? What is its relationship to exegesis on the one hand and systematic theology on the other?

Possible Payoff:

➢ Allows an exploration of one of the most significant questions a biblical scholar might ask: How does a close exegetical analysis of an individual text relate to broader literary, historical, and theological contexts?

➢ Demonstrates that the definitional question is already properly hermeneutical and theological. How one defines BT already assumes how that person conceives of a host of methodological issues (what exegesis entails, the relationship between the testaments, the relevance of theology, etc).

➢ Has direct connection to the issue of practical relevance. How one defines the task of BT will influence whether or not it's seen as useful for the task of ministry among the churches.

Entryway into Scholarship:

Ebeling, Gerhard. "The Meaning of Biblical Theology." In *Journal of Theological Studies* 6.2 (1955): 210–25.

Goldsworthy, Graeme. "Ontology and Biblical Theology." In *Themelios* 28.1 (2002): 37–45.

Klink, Edward and Darian Lockett. *Understanding Biblical Theology: A Comparison of Theory and Practice* (Zondervan, 2012).

Spellman, Ched. "Defining Biblical Theology." Chapter 1 in *Invitation to BT* (Kregel, 2020).

Vos, Gerhardus. "The Idea of BT as a Science and as a Theological Discipline." In *Shorter Writings of Geerhardus Vos* (P&R, 2001), 3–24.

2. Biblical Theology and the Biblical Canon
Canonical Approaches to BT

Starter Questions: What role does the canonical context of the Bible play in the exegesis of individual texts? Is the shape and arrangement of the biblical canon hermeneutically significant? What is a "canonical approach" to BT?

Possible Payoff:

➤ Allows exploration of the relationship between the historical *formation* of the canon and the hermeneutical *function* of the canon.

➤ Highlights that one's basic understanding of the origin and arrangement of the biblical canon does affect certain elements of biblical interpretation (whether consciously or sub-consciously!).

➤ Connects organically to the important issues of authorial intention, the role of the churches as a textual community of biblical readers, and the difference between major ordering traditions in the history of reception (LXX, MT, versions, etc).

Entryway into Scholarship:

Childs, Brevard S. *Biblical Theology of the Old and New Testaments* (Fortress, 1994), esp. pp. 55–94.

Gignilliat, Mark. *Reading the Bible Canonically: Theological Instincts for OT Interpretation* (Baker, 2019).

Glenny, W. and Darian Lockett. *Canon Formation: Tracing the Role of Sub-Collections in the Biblical Canon* (T&T Clark, 2023).

Sailhamer, John. "Biblical Theology and the Composition of the Hebrew Bible." In *Biblical Theology: Retrospect & Prospect* (IVP, 2002), 25–37.

Seitz, Christopher. *The Character of Christian Scripture: The Significance of a Two-Testament Bible* (Baker, 2011).

Spellman, Ched. "Metaphors We Read Canonical Collections By: Exploring the Nature and Effect of Canonical Contextuality." In *JETS* 65.2 (2022): 261–76.

3. The Grand Storyline of the Bible
How the Bible is and is not a "Story"

Starter Questions: Is it proper to speak about the Bible as a "story," and if so, in what way? What are the complicating factors for affirming the presence of a grand storyline that gives coherence to the biblical collection? What is at stake in this discussion?

Possible Payoff:

➢ Forces someone to examine their assumptions about the nature of narrative, the function of overarching theological statements about the Bible, and the hermeneutical issue of unity & diversity.

➢ Considers the possible value of distinguishing and then rightly relating the "many narratives," the "mega-narrative," and the "meta-narrative" of the Bible.

➢ Grapples with the presence of a significant amount of non-narrative books that do not directly connect to the storyline told in the major narrative books of the OT. How is the Bible a story if many parts of the Bible are *not* stories?

Entryway into Scholarship:

Bartholomew, Craig and Mike Goheen. "Story and Biblical Theology." In *Out of Egypt: BT and Biblical Interpretation* (Zondervan, 2004), 144–71.

Bauckham, Richard. "Reading Scripture as a Coherent Story." In *The Art of Reading Scripture* (Eerdmans, 2003), 38–53.

Goheen, Michael. "The Urgency of Reading the Bible as One Story." In *Theology Today* 64 (2008): 469–83.

Lockett, Darian. "Limitations of a Purely Salvation-historical Approach to Biblical Theology." In *Horizons in BT* 39 (2017): 211–31.

Seitz, Christopher. "Can We Read this Book?: Reader Response-ability" and "The Strange Old Book: The Limits of Narrative." Chapters 4–5 in *The Elder Testament* (Baylor, 2018).

4. Biblical Theology and the Covenants
The Nature and Function of the Biblical Covenants

Starter Questions: What is a "biblical covenant," and how do the covenants described in Scripture help us read the Bible as a whole? How are the covenants related to one another? How do the covenants relate to the NT affirmation that Jesus is the Christ?

Possible Payoff:

➢ Explores a concept that is central to many biblical books and the focus of much BT scholarship.

➢ Necessarily joins together the historical, theological, and textual contexts that are operative in biblical interpretation.

➢ Encourages a reader to reckon with the role of the biblical covenants in exegetical analysis, BT reflection, and also systematic theological formulation (particularly within differing comprehensive systems like Covenant Theology or Dispensationalism).

➢ Helps explain the *message* of the grand storyline of the Bible and the distinctive focus of Jesus's teaching and the NT writings.

Entryway into Scholarship:

Gentry, Peter and Stephen Wellum. *God's Kingdom through God's Covenants: A Concise Biblical Theology* (Crossway, 2015).

Parker, Brent and Richard Lucas, ed. *Covenantal and Dispensational Theologies: Four Views on the Continuity of Scripture* (IVP, 2022).

Schreiner, Thomas. *Covenant and God's Purpose for the World* (Crossway, 2017).

Williamson, Paul. *Sealed with an Oath: Covenant in God's Unfolding Purpose* (IVP, 2007).

Orienting Essays: "The Biblical Covenants" (Williamson), "Covenant Theology" (Duncan), and "Progressive Covenantalism & New Covenant Theology" (Wellum) in the TGC Concise Theology series, https://www.thegospelcoalition.org/essay/

5. The "Center" of Biblical Theology:
Arguments for and against Central Themes

Starter Questions: Is there a theme that is so prominent in the Bible that we could call it the "center" of the Bible's message? What would be the criteria for a theme functioning as a "master key" to the theological meaning of all of Scripture? Is this pursuit itself a misguided task?

Possible Payoff:

➤ Informs several parts of one's methodological approach to *discerning* themes in Scripture and also *presenting* those themes.

➤ Recognizes that there are some themes in Scripture that are more prominent than others.

➤ Forces a theologian to grapple with the concepts of both unity and diversity. Is a particular theme a good way to articulate the unity of the Scriptures? Could a "center" do justice to the diversity of genres and distinctive purposes of biblical books?

➤ What is at stake in pursuing a "center" (one theme to rule them all) versus establishing a collection of "central themes" (more of a fellowship of the themes)?

Entryway into Scholarship:

Brendsel, Daniel. "Plots, Themes, and Responsibilities: The Search for a Center of BT Reexamined." In *Themelios* 35.3 (2010): 413–30.

Carson, D.A. "NT Theology." In *Dictionary of the Later NT and its Developments* (IVP, 1997), 796–811.

Rogers, Trent. "Song, Psalm, and Sermon: Toward a Center of Biblical Theology." In *JETS* 64.1 (2021): 129–45.

Sailhamer, John. "Diachronic or Synchronic." Chapter 6 in *Introduction to OT Theology: A Canonical Approach* (Zondervan, 1995).

Spellman, "Tools for Organizing and Presenting BT." Chapter 11 in *Invitation to BT* (Kregel, 2020).

6. Finding Christ in All of Scripture
The Differing Paths to a Christological Reading

Starter Questions: Most evangelical theologians share the theological commitment that the whole Bible speaks in some way of Christ. The hermeneutical question, though, is *how* the whole Bible speaks about Christ. How does the confession that all of Scripture is about Christ relate to the task of BT and the close reading of biblical texts on their own terms?

Possible Payoff:

➢ Strikes at the core confession of Christian theology about Jesus, the gospel message, and the Scriptures.

➢ Must consider the relationship between the testaments and the function of major categories like promise/fulfillment, law/gospel, and prophets/apostles.

➢ Is immediately relevant to the content and emphasis of church ministry (in preaching, teaching, counseling, etc).

➢ Has been directly or indirectly studied and debated in each major era of the history of interpretation.

Entryway into Scholarship:

Alexander, T. Desmond. *From Eden to the New Jerusalem: An Introduction to BT* (Kregel, 2009).

Goldsworthy, Graeme. *According to Plan: The Unfolding Revelation of God in the Bible* (IVP, 2002).

Rydelnik, Michael. *The Messianic Hope: Is the Hebrew Bible Really Messianic?* (B&H, 2010).

Spellman, Ched. "The Bible's Overarching Goal." Chapter 3 in *Invitation to BT* (Kregel, 2020).

Tabb, Brian and Andrew King. *Five Views of Christ in the Old Testament: Genre, Authorial Intent, and the Nature of Scripture* (Zondervan, 2022).

7. Biblical Theology and Interpretive Methods
Typology, Allegory, and Intertextuality

Starter Questions: What is the value of interpretive methods like typology, allegory, and intertextuality? Each of these hermeneutical categories has been utilized by some and also critiqued by other BT practitioners. Each is potentially relevant for BT because of their study of either historical, theological, or literary connections.

Possible Payoff:

➤ Are typology and allegory the same thing? Do these practices have different meanings in different interpretive eras?

➤ How do these interpretive methods relate to an author's textual intention? Is typology, allegory, or intertextuality a feature of an author's strategy or something that is theologically embedded and retrospectively perceived by readers?

➤ What are the criteria that would justify confidence in a given typological, allegorical, or intertextual connection?

➤ Are these interpretive tools mutually exclusive? Is one more prominent across the biblical canon than the others?

Entryway into Scholarship:

Chase, Mitchell. *40 Questions about Typology and Allegory* (Kregel, 2020).

Hamilton, James. *Typology: Understanding the Bible's Promise-Shaped Patterns* (Zondervan, 2022).

Hoskins, Paul. *That Scripture Might Be Fulfilled: Typology and the Death of Christ* (Xulon, 2009).

Smith, Brandon. *Taught by God: Ancient Hermeneutics for the Modern Church* (B&H, 2024).

Spellman, Ched. "Intertextuality within the Canonical Context." Chapter 4 in *Toward a Canon-Conscious Reading of the Bible* (Sheffield-Phoenix, 2014).

8. Biblical Theology and the Great Tradition
Exploring Precursors to the Discipline of BT

Starter Questions: What are the precursors to the modern discipline of BT? Is it even proper to speak of "biblical theology" before the modern era? What are the significant lines of continuity and discontinuity between BT and the interpretive approaches of theologians in different historical eras?

Possible Payoff:

➤ Potentially demonstrates that contemporary BT has roots that predate the priorities and challenges of the modern period.

➤ Explores the riches of the history of interpretation on some of the same questions that BT grapples with (the relationship b/w the testaments, Christ in the OT, the place of the law in the new covenant, etc).

➤ Helps contemporary interpreters recognize the influence that previous generations of biblical readers have had on both our hermeneutical questions and answers.

Entryway into Scholarship:

Childs, Brevard S. *The Struggle to Understand Isaiah as Christian Scripture* (Eerdmans, 2004).

Hall, Christopher. *Reading Scripture with the Church Fathers* (IVP, 1998).

Marsh, William M. *Martin Luther on Reading the Bible as Christian Scripture* (Wipf & Stock, 2017).

Presley, Stephen. *Biblical Theology in the Life of the Early Church: Recovering an Ancient Vision* (Baker, 2025).

Scobie, Charles. "History of Biblical Theology." In *New Dictionary of Biblical Theology* (IVP, 2000), 11–20.

Glossary of Key Terms

Advent—the coming of Christ; the season in the "church calendar" that prepares for the celebration of Christmas.

Biblical theology—the careful study of the whole Bible on its own terms.

Canon—a way of referring to the Bible; a term that combines the sense of "normative rule" and "ordered collection." In reference to the Bible, the authoritative collection of authoritative biblical writings.

Canon-consciousness—the awareness of a canonical collection or the authority of a group of writings; can refer either to a biblical author or a biblical reader.

Canonical approach—an approach to biblical studies that focuses on the final form of biblical texts and considers the association and arrangement of biblical books within a collection to have hermeneutical significance.

Central theme—a theme in Scripture that shows up and develops across the biblical canon; a theme that helps show how the Bible fits together.

Compositional approach—an approach to reading the Bible that examines how authors composed their texts in order to discern how best to read those same texts.

Compositional strategy—the purpose of an author that can be discerned in the way they have composed their text; seen through editorial comments, through the shape or structure of a work, and through discernible literary patterns; interchangeable with "textual strategy."

Confessional approach—an approach to reading the Bible that acknowledges and builds upon a set of theological presuppositions about God, the Bible, and biblical readers.

Covenant—a relationship based on a promise; usually with an expectation of blessings for obedience and curses for disobedience.

Eisegesis—To push the meaning "into" (*eis-*) a text; usually only used in a pejorative sense; importing an exegetical conclusion or a theological meaning into a text that conflicts with "the way the words go."

Exegesis— To draw the meaning "out of" (*ex-*) a text; the close reading of a particular textual unit (or biblical passage); the study of an author's textual intent.

Incomprehensibility—the belief that it is ultimately not possible to exhaustively comprehend God's being and character; a feature of God's infinite nature and humanity's finite nature.

Inner-textuality—the study of literary connections and textual patterns that occur within the confines of a single work.

Inter-textuality—the study of the relationship between two or more texts. An umbrella term that usually encompasses direct quotations, indirect allusions, and more subtle literary echoes of other texts.

Kerygma—a term that refers to the "preached word" of the apostles in the earliest churches; the content of the gospel message and also the proclamation of that gospel message.

Knowability—the belief that it is possible to know God adequately because of the general and special revelation of God himself.

Lament—a prayer to God that includes both an acknowledgement of pain or complaint alongside an affirmation of trust; a poetic genre that includes these elements.

Liturgy—a repeated practice that is intended to communicate meaning; usually refers to the ordering of a corporate worship service.

Mega-narrative—the "biblical mega-narrative" (or the grand storyline of the Bible) is the larger narrative framework that arises when the many narratives of the Bible are understood to be part of a single coherent collection of truthful texts.

Memento mori—a phrase that means "remember death" and refers to the practice of remembering that humans are finite and that our life will inevitably come to an end; usually also functions as a means of remembering to trust in the Lord.

Messiah/Christ—a term meaning "anointed one." Usually associated in biblical texts with the coming descendant of David who would rule with righteousness and establish God's kingdom.

Meta-narrative—the "biblical meta-narrative" is the set of assumptions that are generated by the grand storyline of the Bible (the "mega-narrative"); the theological commitments that follow from accepting the truth of the Bible's meaning (a Christian "worldview").

Ordinary time—the stretch of weeks in the "church calendar" between Pentecost Sunday and the first week of Advent.

Pentateuch—a term for the first five books of the OT (Genesis, Exodus, Leviticus, Numbers, and Deuteronomy); a way of referring to the book of Moses as a single, five-part work rather than five discrete books.

Theology—the study of God and all things in relation to God according to his word; sometimes used interchangeably with "systematic theology" in distinction from "biblical theology."

Acknowledgements and Dedication

Acknowledgments
Special thanks to my lovely Leigh Anne and our precious Hope, Kate, Luke, and Claire. Y'all are my favorite theologians to learn from. My six-year-old Claire was an exacting editor and declared at several points in her perusal of the manuscript page proofs that "nope, this is not going to work, cut all these words out at once!!" I'm sure there will be readers who will wish that I had followed her advice more often.

I'm also thankful for the opportunity to have taught and developed this material for the past decade with students training for ministry in Hermeneutics, Biblical Theology, and Bible & the Gospel courses. Heaps of gratitude as well for colleagues and students who have read portions of this material and offered helpful feedback and encouraging words (even those that have abandoned me to go teach in other states): Zach Bowden, Jarrett Ford, JR Gilhooly, Jason Lee, Billy Marsh, Brandon Smith, Jonathan Watson; Luke Brittan, and Deborah Honeycutt.

Dedication
This volume is warmly dedicated to my mom, Janet Spellman. The apostle Paul once encouraged Timothy to persevere in the faith and continue in what he had learned (2 Tim 3:14).

He also calls Timothy to remember one of the special blessings God had given him: "From childhood you have been acquainted with the sacred writings, which are able to make you wise for salvation through faith in Christ Jesus" (2 Tim 3:15). One of my first memories of prayer is when Mom asked the Lord to make my headache go away during an evening church service. She was also there years later one night as I asked Christ to save me after being convicted by a gospel message.

This little book is about the text of Scripture and the big picture of the Bible. My first memories of the words of Scripture are in her voice. Growing up, I wasn't always sure of myself, but because of her I always knew that I was "fearfully and wonderfully made" (Ps 139:14). Some days were good, some days were sad. But I knew that this is a day "that the Lord has made," and so we can still rejoice and be glad in it (Ps 118:24). I can remember being fearful, but I can also hear her gentle but absolutely confident reminder that "greater is he that is in you, than he that is in the world" (1 Jn 4:4).

Because of her love and guidance, "from childhood" I have been "acquainted with the sacred writings." She often prays that the Lord might "bless and keep" me, and her faithful legacy is one of the means by which God has done this for me. This is a gift that can only be repaid with gratitude. *Thanks, Mom!*

Selected Scripture Index

Old Testament
Genesis
book of..............5, 13
1–11.......................40
1–3...................46, 58,
63, 106, 130
1:1.....................14, 40,
45, 51, 104
1:26–31.....................58
2:15...........14, 58, 106
5:1–2.................64, 76
6–9............................58
9:6–7.......................64
12...............40, 58, 69
15:1–21...................58
37–50.....................40
49.......55, 56, 110, 112
Exodus
book of 63
12:46.......................98
19–24...........17, 54, 58
20.............................40
26.............................45
34.............................27
Leviticus
book of...................63
Numbers
book of...................63
3:7–8......................112
9:12..........................98
10.............................40
24:7–9...................110
Deuteronomy
book of........40, 63, 78
5...............................54
6:20–25...................65
7–8............................9
11:1–17....................65
18:15–19................69
26:5–9......................65
27–33.....................55
29:29.......................20
29–30.....................56

30–34 .... 17, 56
30:6–10 58
Joshua
23–24 55
24:1–15 65
Judges
2:1–5 65
1 Samuel
12–13 .... 55, 65
2 Samuel
7:8–17 .... 58, 110
1 Kings
2 55
2 Kings
17 .... 55, 56
25 55
Nehemiah
9:5–37 65
1 Chronicles
1–9 .... 41, 75
1:1 41
17 58
23:32 112
Psalms
book of 42
2:7 .... 29, 77,
81, 85, 111
8 82
16:10 85
22 ...... 96–97, 111, 136
23:1 .... 51, 136
34:20 98
39 129–30
42 140
69 97
78 65
90 130
105–06 65
110:1, 4 .... 81, 85
118 92
119:68 13
135–36 65

145:17......................13
145:3.......................21
Ecclesiastes
1:2–4......................130
12:1–13.................130
Isaiah
11:1–10..................112
40:3..........................29
42:1....................29, 77
43:7.........................14
43:16–21.................54
49:6.........................85
55:3.........................85
61:10......................112
Jeremiah
book of....................13
2:1–13......................65
31:31–35............58, 60
36:1–32..................17
Lamentations
3:21–42..................137
5:21–22..................137
Ezekiel
20.............................65
34:5.........................29
36:22–32.................58
37:24–28...............100
40–48.....................112
44:14......................112
Daniel
12:1–2...................114
Joel
2:28–32................85
Amos
2:6–3:2..................65
Jonah
1–3......................27, 36
4................................36
4:1–3.......................27
Micah
6:1–8.......................65

Nahum
1:7 51
Habakkuk
1:5 85
Zechariah
9–13 92–96
Malachi
3:1 29
New Testament
Matthew
book of 42, 74
1–4 74–77
1:1 .... 18, 29,
            60, 75–76, 88
1:1–25 ... 65, 75–76, 85
4:23 18
9:25 18
12:23 99
13:44 1
13:52 146
26:13 18
26:28 60
27 99
28:20 .... 42, 55
Mark
book of 42
1:1 .... 19, 42
1:2 29
1:4–8 18
1:11 .... 18, 29
1:13 29
1:15 19
Luke
book of 42
9:22 147
22:20 60
24 .... 55, 64,
            148, 152–53
John
book of 42, 87ff
1:1–2 88
1:10 91
1:14 88
1:43–51 91
6:39–40 114
10:1–30 94–96

11 115–16
12 92–93
13:36 113
14:5 113
16:33 51
18–19 89–99
20:30–31 .... 88, 99
21:24–25 18
Acts
1 55
2:14–21 .... 68–69, 85
2:32–33 122
13:13–41 .... 69, 85
6–7 .... 55, 65
8:30–31 143
17 151–52
20 55
27 45
28 .... 45, 55
Romans
book of 5, 63
1:1–4 69
6:3–11 122
8 .... 123, 139
15:12 112
1 Corinthians
11:25 60
15:3–4 .... 18, 70
15:12–57 116
2 Corinthians
4:4 64
4:7–9 138
5:1–10 138
6:10 127
Galatians
book of 13, 63
Ephesians
1:9–10 14
5:15–21 124–25
Colossians
1:15 64
3:9–10 64
1 Thessalonians
2:13 18
4:13–16 117

2 Thessalonians
3:8–16 121
1 Timothy
3:16 118
2 Timothy
2:1–8 70–71
3:14–17 16
Titus
2:13 100
Hebrews
book of 63, 78
1:1–4 78–80
1:1 21
1:3 64
1:5–14 81
2:8–10 80
3–4 80
3:1–6 80
4:1–10 85
5:5 81
7:1–10 85
8–10 .... 58, 82
11 .... 65, 85
11:3 14
12:18–29 80
James
book of 63
3:9 64
4:13–15 131
2 Peter
1:16–21 16
3:15–16 18
Revelation
book of 6, 104–11
1:1–3 149
11:15 111
12:9 112
20:2, 10 112
21–22 .... 46, 55,
            104–11, 139, 149

General Index

Alexander, T. Desmond, 161, 168
Auerbach, Eric, 51
Bartholomew, Craig, 166
Bauckham, Richard, 166
Beale, G.K., 161
Bowden, Zach, 175
Brendsel, Daniel, 168
Bruno, Christopher, 65
Caravaggio, Michelangelo, 153–54, 156
Carey, William, 119
Carson, D.A., 161, 168
Chase, Mitchell, 170
Childs, Brevard, 165, 171
Cline, Robert, 162
Compton, Jared, 65
de Champaigne, Philippe, 141
Dempster, Stephen, 49, 51
Duncan, Ligon, 167
Ebeling, Gerhard, 164
Every day, *see Roman Empire*
Ford, Jarrett, 175
Frodo, 103
Gignilliat, Mark, 165
Gilhooly, JR, 175
Gentry, Peter, 167
Gladd, Benjamin, 161
Glenny, W. Edward, 165
Goheen, Mike, 166
Goldsworthy, Graeme, 164, 168
Hafemann, Scott, 161
Hall, Christopher, 171
Hamilton, James, 162, 170
Hoskins, Paul, 170
King, Andrew, 169
Klink, Edward, 162, 164
Irenaeus, 20, 22
Lawrence, Michael, 162
Lee, Jason, 175
Lewis, C.S., 143

Lockett, Darian, 162, 164, 165, 166
Lucas, Richard, 167
Marsh, William M., 171, 175
Mather, Cotton, 133, 141
McCullough, Matthew, 141
McFadden, Kevin, 65
Naselli, Andrew, 161
Parker, Brent, 167
Presley, Stephen, 171
Rembrandt, 154–55, 156
Ricoeur, Paul, 127
Roark, Elisabeth, 141
Roark, Nick, 162
Rogers, Trent, 168
Roman Empire, 24, see also *every day*
Rosner, Brian, 161
Rublev, Andrei, 154
Rydelnik, Michael, 169
Sailhamer, John, 51, 112, 162, 165, 168
Schaeffer, Francis, 15
Schreiner, Thomas, 162, 167
Scobie, Charles, 171
Seitz, Christopher, 165, 166
Shakespeare, William, 128
Shepherd, Michael, 65
Smaug, 1, 2
Smith, Brandon, 170, 175
Spurgeon, Charles H., 32–35, 37
Stannard, David, 141
Tabb, Brian, 169
Tanner, Henry Ossawa, 155–56
Tolkien, J. R. R., 1
Vanhoozer, Kevin, 51, 141
Vos, Gerhardus, 164
Watson, Jonathan, 175
Wellum, Stephen, 167
Williamson, Paul, 167
xkcd, 37

Τετέλεσται

Made in the USA
Monee, IL
20 April 2025

15952968R00111